Sexual Harassment:

A Guide to a Harassment-Free Workplace

By Kathleen Kapusta, J.D.

Wolters Kluwer

This publication is designed to provide accurate and authoritative information in regard to the subject matter covered. It is sold with the understanding that the publisher is not engaged in rendering legal, accounting, or other professional service. If legal advice or other expert assistance is required, the services of a competent professional person should be sought.

978-1-5438-0528-4

2700 Lake Cook Road
Riverwoods, IL 60015
1 866 529 6600
www.WoltersKluwerLR.com

Contents

CHAPTER 1: Why worry about sexual harassment?

Why worry about sexual harassment?......................................1

Costs of harassment 3

    Hidden costs 4

    Litigation costs 4

    Mandatory arbitration 5

    Damages...6

The culture is changing...8

Employer's role in preventing harassment 9

CHAPTER 2: What is sexual harassment?

Introduction 13

Unwelcome sexual conduct..14

    Guard against "tolerated" behavior 16

Hostile work environment sexual harassment 17

    What is hostile?..18

    Are compliments wrong? 20

    Isolated incidents..21

Participation in the conduct 21

Quid pro quo sexual harassment 24

Same-sex and sexual orientation harassment................................25

Nonemployee harassment...27

Off-work conduct..28

Workplace romances...29

    Take workplace romances seriously 33

CHAPTER 3: Employer liability

Liability standards..36

Alter ego harassment 36

    Top executives set the tone 37

    The risk is substantial 38

Supervisor harassment...40

    Job action taken—automatic liability 40

    No tangible job action—limited defense 41

Has #MeToo changed the perception of what is reasonable,
both for employers and employees? 44
        Personal liability...48
Coworker sexual harassment 48
        Knowledge 48
        Stopping the harassment 49
Nonemployee harassment...51
Monitoring manager and supervisors 54

CHAPTER 4: Policy creation and communication

Why have a policy? 56
Key provisions 57
        Define sexual harassment..58
        Complaint procedure 60
        Protection from retaliation......................................66
        Prompt investigation 67
        Confidentiality 68
        Disciplining the offender..69
Communicating the policy..70
        Distribute and post..70
        Train...72
        Get acknowledgement 72

CHAPTER 5: Sexual harassment training

Why hasn't sexual harassment training worked?..........................75
Training overview...76
Traditional compliance training 78
Bystander intervention training 80
Workplace civility training 83
When to train 85
Who to train 86
Evaluation..87
Changing the culture..87

CHAPTER 6: Investigating harassment

Becoming aware of harassment 89
The initial complaint...91
        The reluctant employee...92
        The delayed complaint 93
        The top performer 95

Starting the investigation. 96
    What are the steps? 96
    Who should investigate? 97
Obtaining relevant information 99
Conducting the interviews 100
    The complainant. 100
    Other witnesses 104
    The accused 105
    Determining credibility 108
Documenting the process 111
Maintaining confidentiality 112
    Understanding and avoiding defamation 113
Protecting the accuser and the accused
during the investigation 115

CHAPTER 7: Resolution and corrective action

Making a determination 118
    The hard-to-resolve claim. 118
Taking prompt action 120
    Notice of resolution 124
Addressing the victim 124
    Transfers and reassignments 125
    The false complaint 125
Disciplining the offender 126
    Be consistent. 129
Addressing the workforce. 129
Preventing retaliation. 129
Documenting the process 131
Following up 132
Use of nondisclosure agreements 133
Corrective action and the corporate culture 134

Chapter 1

Why worry about sexual harassment?

In the past two weeks, two managers have come to you concerned about possible workplace sexual harassment situations. One manager overheard a sexually charged conversation between a mixed group of workers, while the other saw a male employee touching a female coworker on the shoulder and saying she looked "hot," while she "looked uncomfortable." Nobody has complained to either manager about potential harassment. Of course, this could not have happened at a worse time. The organization is currently going through a reorganization and you're completely swamped with documentation and meetings. In addition, the HR office is understaffed and overworked due to a recent downsizing. What responsibility does HR have to take measures that will help prevent sexual harassment from occurring? How are employers expected to respond if sexual harassment is observed? If you choose to wait until your time frees up to do anything about the potential harassment, what's the worst that could happen? After all, nobody is complaining, right?

Why worry about sexual harassment?

After multiple accusations of sexual harassment and assault against a famous Hollywood producer forced him out of his own company in late 2017, the #MeToo movement took hold. It exploded a short time later when person after person stepped forward with back-to-back allegations of sexual harassment in virtually every corner of the American workplace. Employers large and small were left reeling as these accusations revealed entrenched sexual harassment, prompted very public investigations, and toppled employees and CEOs alike.

Because sexual harassment may often be subtle or hidden, it is not always easy for employers to spot and effectively deal with it when it occurs. However, managers and supervisors who engage in sexual harassment subject their employers to automatic liability, regardless of whether management or HR condones the conduct or are even aware of it. Nonsupervisory employees who engage in harassment can also subject their employers to liability if HR or management knows or should know about the conduct and fails to take prompt action to stop it. Negative publicity, the high cost of turnover, lowered employee morale, and the potential costs associated with lawsuits are just some of the devastating effects sexual harassment can have on the workplace.

The changing workplace. The makeup of the workplace itself may contribute to an increased likelihood of sexual harassment. The so-called "gig economy," and its addition of more temporary, flexible jobs, an influx of contractors, and more fluid, less physically segregated environments, are just some of the many changes that have impacted the modern workplace, presenting new and different challenges for HR. These changes to the traditional office environment "are both good and bad in terms of sexual harassment prevention," observes Sherman and Howard attorney Brooke Colaizzi, noting that employers have less control over employees who are not in the office from 9-5 and less ability to control the overall working environment, including monitoring how the workforce interacts.

Employees who have more freedom to work remotely on their own time and in their own environments might not feel as trapped by a difficult or abusive work environment, Colaizzi observed. On the other hand, she suggested, "cube farms," as opposed to the more traditional closed-in offices, promote more frequent worker interaction, which in turn may lead to an increased potential for harassment.

What about the gig economy and the increased use of contractors by employers? These workers, Chris Bourgeacq of the Chris Bourgeacq Law Firm pointed out, "will likely find it more difficult to pursue statutory discrimination claims against their attackers due to the limited application of Title VII and state counterparts to nonemployees."

Other problematic workplaces. Other workplaces may give rise to a greater likelihood of sexual harassment as well. An isolated workplace may not only increase the difficulty in reporting harassment, it may make policy enforcement more difficult. Further, as women continue to move into male-dominated occupations, employers should at the very least be prepared for a potential increase in incidents of sexual harassment.

And as Colaizzi pointed out, "workplaces that include individuals with significant amounts of wealth, power, and/or fame may have a higher incidence of sexual harassment or a greater likelihood that sexual harassment will go unreported."

HR's best defense is an offense. What can companies do to prevent and eliminate what has proven to be such an enduring workplace problem? Creating, communicating, and strictly enforcing a strong culture and policy against sexual harassment and other inappropriate conduct is a must, but it is only the beginning. HR should take all allegations seriously, never dismiss a complaint as trivial, and swiftly address the complaint or otherwise take action to stop the conduct.

Maintaining the right workplace culture

Employers have sought to prevent harassment through a variety of mechanisms, including disseminating policies and training employees, according to Jackson Lewis attorney Stephanie Adler-Paindiris, who suggests that employers ensure:

- Leaders are modeling the correct behavior (it starts at the top);
- The proper message is repeatedly communicated to employees;
- They immediately and thoroughly manage situations when they arise; and
- They are monitoring to ensure that their preventive practices, including policy dissemination and training, are actually working to prevent harassment.

Costs of harassment

While lawsuits are certainly one very good reason why HR should be doing all that it can to stop sexual harassment—in 2017 alone, the EEOC received over 12,000 charges alleging sex-based harassment—they are not the only reason. In today's highly competitive global market, there are also hidden costs that may prove to be more expensive than a lawsuit.

These include lowered morale, lost productivity, and harm to an organization's reputation.

Hidden costs

Lost productivity and lowered morale. Workplace sexual harassment will cost an employer lost productive time. Not only can harassment limit the victim's ability to contribute to the organization, other employees who observe or learn about the harassment are likely also to be negatively affected. If HR does nothing to address the problem, it can become demoralizing to employees and potentially lead to increased absenteeism and turnover.

Harm to reputation. Especially following allegations against high-profile media and government leaders in 2017 and 2018, sexual harassment cases more often than not attract media attention, elevating the matter into a high-profile problem. When harassment claims become public, the employer's reputation in the community suffers, business opportunities may be lost, and good applicants may avoid seeking employment with the organization. Current employees may seek other opportunities, too.

> **Don't miss this!** *The internal reputation of the organization also suffers. An employer that allows harassment to occur is, in effect, undermining its vision, its mission, and its core values. After all, an employer can hardly claim that "our people are our most important asset," yet allow sexual harassment and other inappropriate behavior to occur unchecked.*

Litigation costs

Defending a sexual harassment lawsuit can be prohibitively expensive. Because of the high costs associated with going to trial, it is simply bad business sense for employers not to take proactive measures to prevent and eliminate sexual harassment in the workplace. Two of the highest costs associated with litigation are the costs associated with settling a complaint and the cost of taking a case to trial.

Settlements. In order to prevent harm to business and personal reputations, and to avoid the possibility of a multi-million-dollar damage award if a victim sues and wins, employers often settle sexual harassment claims. Sometimes, parties hire a mediator to help negotiate a settlement. The mediator's fees, in addition to the organization's attorneys' fees, can really add up. In short, settlements can be quite expensive compared to the cost of taking proactive steps to prevent sexual harassment.

Mandatory arbitration

In an attempt to avoid some of the costs associated with litigation and settlement, as well as to diminish the reputational harms that may result from highly public legal proceedings, many employers require their employees, as a condition of employment, to sign arbitration agreements mandating that sexual harassment claims be resolved through confidential arbitration instead of judicial proceedings. These employers include mandatory arbitration of employment disputes as a part of their employment relationships, requiring employees to agree to arbitration instead of litigation because, they believe, arbitration is faster, more efficient, less costly, and more *private*.

On the other hand, some prominent advocates in the #MeToo movement are arguing that sexual harassment claims in particular should not be subject to mandatory arbitration—and are urging that the law should be changed to prevent it. Why? In a letter to Congressional leadership from the National Association of Attorneys General, signed by the chief legal officers of the states, District of Columbia, and territories, they signaled they "strongly support appropriately-tailored legislation to ensure that sexual harassment victims have a right to their day in court."

The theory is that "victims of such serious misconduct" shouldn't have to rely on "decision makers who are not trained as judges, are not qualified to act as courts of law," and who don't ensure "due process." Plus, they identified concerns about the "secrecy requirements of arbitration clauses," which keep both the harassment complaints and any settlements confidential," and may prevent other victims from realizing they are not alone.

> **Don't miss this!** *Just a few months after former Fox News anchor Gretchen Carlson initially filed a sexual harassment lawsuit, 21st Century Fox announced that it had settled her claims for $20 million. The network even offered her a public apology. That $20 million settlement is not the biggest settlement, though; former Fox News host Bill O'Reilly reportedly settled sexual harassment allegations for $32 million in October 2017. Of course, not all settlement amounts would be reported publicly in any event, as some parties make nondisclosure a condition of settling a sexual harassment case—for any amount.*

Costs of going to trial. Regardless of whether an employer wins or loses a sexual harassment lawsuit, it may spend hundreds of thousands of dollars defending the case. Attorneys' fees, which generally are borne by the organization regardless of whether it wins or loses, fees paid to expert witnesses, and the costs of discovery can all negatively impact an employer's bottom line. Indeed, the high cost of litigation is often the motivation for settling a case, even when an employer believes it has a strong defense.

> **Example:** *According to The 2017 Hiscox Guide to Employee Lawsuits: "A representative study of 1,214 closed claims reported by small-to-medium-sized enterprises with fewer than 500 employees showed that 24 percent of employment charges resulted in defense and settlement costs averaging a total of $160,000. On average, those matters took 318 days to resolve. The average employer's self-insured retention deductible for these charges was $50,000. Without employment practices liability insurance, each of these companies would have been out of pocket by an extra $110,000 on average."*

Damages

Above and beyond the costs of going to trial are the monetary damages that an organization will be forced to pay if it loses a lawsuit.

Types of damages. An employer that loses a sexual harassment suit may be ordered to pay the victim:

- Back wages for any lost time at work as a result of the harassment.
- Reimbursement for any monetary losses (for example, doctor's bills or money spent seeking another job).
- Compensatory damages for emotional harm suffered as a result of the harassment (including mental anguish, loss of enjoyment of life, and inconvenience), as well as future monetary losses (such as those expected due to inability to work or future medical expenses).
- Punitive damages to punish the organization for any wrongdoing.
- Future wages (if reinstatement is not feasible under the circumstances).
- The victim's attorneys' fees and costs.

✔ CHECKLIST: Determining punitive damages

Courts generally will look at the following factors in deciding whether an employer found liable for sexual harassment should pay punitive damages:

- ☐ The nature and severity of the harassment;
- ☐ The nature, extent, and severity of harm to the victim;
- ☐ The duration of the harassment;
- ☐ The existence and frequency of previous harassment;
- ☐ Evidence that the employer planned or attempted to cover up the harassment;
- ☐ The employer's actions after it became aware of the harassment; and
- ☐ Whether the victim was threatened or retaliated against for complaining to management or for filing an EEOC charge.

What kind of money are we talking? Like most legal questions, the answer is "it depends." Although employers have, in some cases, been ordered to pay monetary damages in the millions of dollars, more often damages will range in the hundreds of thousands of dollars.

Worst case scenario

According to multiple media sources, the biggest reported jury verdict for a single individual in a sexual harassment lawsuit went to a cardiac surgery physician's assistant in 2012. That award was $168 million, which included punitive damages. The woman claimed doctors at Mercy General Hospital constantly asked her for sex, and when she complained, her supervisor would "just laugh." She also complained about workplace conditions and patient safety, complaints that allegedly resulted in her firing. Her lawyer called the hospital a "raunchy, vile, toxic workplace" and the environment "bullying and inappropriate."

The year before, an employee at a rent-to-own store reportedly was awarded $95 million as the result of allegations that the general manager sexually assaulted her after harassing her for a year. He was arrested that same day. She said that she called a company hotline five months before the assault, but an investigator never contacted her. Instead, her complaint alleged the general manager's supervisor later confronted her, in the presence of the general manager, and warned the general manager to "watch his back" because of her complaint.

The $95 million verdict was later reduced to $40 million because of a cap on federal damages.

The culture is changing

By 2018, the complacency of the culture towards sexual harassment was undergoing significant change. For example, an article from December 2017 in voanews.com noted that "By the end of 2017, more than 60 prominent men were suspended, fired or forced to resign from their highly visible jobs because of allegations of sexual harassment and even assault against women, some occurring years ago. More than 100 stand accused of sexual harassment or misconduct."

The article went on to note the influence of social media: "#MeToo became the rallying cry for women worldwide. Women posted the hashtag on Twitter and Facebook to acknowledge publicly their experiences and to demonstrate the extent of the problem. Time magazine named 'The Silence Breakers' as its 'Person of the Year' for 2017. The issue is dedicated to those who have accused powerful figures of sexual misconduct, calling them the 'voices that launched a movement.'"

Think back to the two managers who told you about the potentially harassing situations. As you can see, while doing nothing was never acceptable, doing nothing in the age of #MeToo and enhanced awareness and media attention may prove quite costly. It is imperative that HR investigate each incident to determine whether sexual harassment is occurring so that appropriate action can be taken to restore a harassment-free environment. The need to address potential workplace harassment may mean appealing to upper-level management for additional resources. Or, it may mean putting other tasks on the back burner in order to focus on promptly investigating and resolving the reported incidents.

Choosing to ignore the potential harassment, however, could end up being a very costly mistake.

Employer's role in preventing harassment

Clearly, the interests of both employers and employees are best served when sexual harassment is prevented from ever becoming a problem in the first place. How HR creates a diverse, inclusive, and respectful culture, and prevents and reacts to sexual harassment in the workplace will play an important role in helping an employer avoid both the legal and hidden costs of harassment.

★ Best practices

The following guidelines can help reduce and possibly avoid the chance of sexual harassment occurring in your organization:

1. **Issue a strong policy against sexual harassment.** As a part of creating a culture of respect, write the policy so that all employees can understand it. Define and provide examples of sexual harassment in all kinds of positions that make up your organization, and make the explanation of prohibited conduct very clear. Explain the disciplinary sanctions up to and including discharge that will be applied to harassers, and reassure anyone who reports harassment that he or she will be protected from retaliation.

2. **Outline a complaint procedure.** Make it easy for employees to report sexual harassment. Provide multiple avenues of reporting so that the employee has the ability to bypass his or her supervisor, or even HR, or anyone who might be the alleged harasser.

3. **Communicate the policy.** Distribute and regularly and clearly communicate the policy to all employees; document that you have done so. Redistribute the policy periodically, especially the channels for reporting harassment. Post the policy in central locations, on your organization's intranet if applicable, and incorporate it into employee handbooks, both print and on-line versions.

4. **Train employees.** Educate all employees, including supervisory staff and management, to recognize and confront sexual harassment. Emphasize their responsibility to report harassment should it happen to them—or if they witness it—and explain how they should do so. Keep records of attendance at training sessions.

5. **Train managers and supervisors.** Supervisory staff and management should receive additional training on how to enforce the policy and to be sensitive and responsive to improper conduct. Instruct all supervisors and managers to address or report all complaints of sexual harassment, even if the complaint does not conform to the complaint procedures, or even if the complaint involves conduct that happened years ago.

6. **Monitor managers and supervisors.** Include EEO preventative practices in a manager's or supervisor's job responsibilities. Monitor their conduct to make sure these folks are carrying out their responsibilities to support and maintain an environment free of harassment.

7. **Investigate every complaint.** Do not assume that any complaint is not important. All sexual harassment claims, even anonymous ones or ones that involve conduct from years ago, must be taken seriously and investigated promptly and thoroughly by an impartial investigator. Investigators should be well trained in the skills required for interviewing witnesses and evaluating credibility.

8. **Maintain confidentiality.** Maintaining confidentiality assists in encouraging employees to come forward with complaints; it also reduces the risk of a defamation lawsuit.

9. **Act immediately to stop harassment.** Correct apparent harassment, regardless of whether a complaint has been filed. Adopt a remedy that will be effective to end the harassment. Restore any job benefits or opportunities to the victim that were lost because of the harassment, and offer appropriate counseling or other compensation for losses. Discipline the harasser in a manner that reflects the severity of the conduct.

10. **Follow up periodically.** It is important that the remedy effectively stops the harassment and that no retaliation has been taken against the victim or any witnesses. You won't know whether this is true unless you follow up

11. **Document the investigation.** Develop and keep accurate records of all details of a harassment investigation. Preserve the complete record in a safe, confidential manner for a period of time that is at least as long as any regulatory or state statute of limitations that may apply.

12. **Stop retaliation immediately.** Failure to stop retaliation against an employee who complains of harassment or someone who participates in a sexual harassment investigation can result in liability for an employer, regardless of the outcome of the investigation itself. The employer should follow up periodically to ensure the retaliation does not occur again.

Don't miss this! *The success of prevention efforts "depends in large part on employer culture," notes Brooke Colaizzi, observing that because some environments are more conducive to complaints about sexual harassment, "it is important for an employer to recognize what kind of environment exists and to keep tabs on the ebbs and flows of that environment." Chris Bourgeacq suggests that employers ensure employees know the following about their particular workplace:*

- *There's a policy against sexual harassment and they can understand it.*
- *They have a process to report sexual harassment, anonymously if need be.*
- *Their report will be promptly investigated.*
- *They will not be retaliated against for filing a report.*
- *The employer will take prompt remedial action.*

Chapter 2

What is sexual harassment?

Seth, one of the managers at your organization, stops by your office. He just finished speaking to Jennifer, an employee who approached him with a complaint of sexual harassment. Jennifer told Seth that two of her male coworkers, Roger and Juan, often make off-color, sexual jokes in her presence. She also told him they make comments about the appearance of other women in the office. Jennifer said that this conduct makes her feel uncomfortable and she doesn't know what to do. Seth informs you that he has spoken briefly to Roger and Juan and they admitted they sometimes joke around but claimed they had no idea Jennifer was upset. In fact, according to the two men, Jennifer often comments on her own sex life in response to their questions. Could Jennifer be a victim of sexual harassment? Does it matter whether Jennifer did in fact join in the sexual banter? What should you do next?

Introduction

Despite corporate America's embrace of preventative measures—as the #MeToo movement clearly revealed—keeping the workplace free of inappropriate sexual behavior continues to be a challenge for employers. Why is sexual harassment so persistent? One reason, suggests FisherBroyles attorney Eric Meyer is that "some employers are not proactive enough to implement prophylactic steps (e.g., training, handbook updates) to educate employees and managers about the scourge of sexual harassment." And even "the best workplaces with the most training will have 'rogue' individuals engaging in bad behavior regardless of the number of safeguards that may exist."

According to the EEOC, the federal agency that enforces federal laws against employment discrimination, sexual harassment can occur in a variety of circumstances:

- The victim as well as the harasser may be a woman or a man. The victim does not have to be of the opposite sex.
- The harasser can be the victim's supervisor, an agent of the employer, a supervisor in another area, a coworker, or even a nonemployee.
- The victim does not have to be the person harassed—but could be anyone affected by the offensive conduct.
- Unlawful sexual harassment may occur without economic injury to or discharge of the victim.
- The harasser's conduct must be unwelcome, however.

Unwelcome sexual conduct

Sexual harassment is a form of sex discrimination, which is specifically prohibited by federal and state law. Sexual harassment in the workplace occurs when an employee is made to feel uncomfortable because of unwelcome sexual conduct. It includes unwelcome sexual advances, requests for sexual favors, and other verbal or physical conduct of a sexual nature. Because it is often subtle, it is not always easy to decide whether sexual harassment has occurred or to effectively deal with it when it does occur.

How much harassment is there? In the report of its Select Task Force on the Study of Harassment in the Workplace published in June 2016, the EEOC said that it learned that anywhere from 25 percent to 85 percent of women report having experienced sexual harassment in the workplace. What can we make of these widely divergent percentages? The Commission, too, tried to understand what these numbers could tell us about the scope of harassment based on sex.

When it is labeled "sexual harassment." The EEOC found that when employees were asked, in surveys using a randomly representative sample (a probability sample), if they had experienced "sexual harassment," without that term being defined in the survey, approximately one in four women (25%) reported experiencing "sexual harassment" in the workplace, a percentage "remarkably consistent" across probability surveys. When employees were asked the same question in surveys using convenience samples (one that is not randomly representative because it uses respondents that are convenient to the researcher, like students or volunteers), with sexual harassment not being defined, the rate rose to 50 percent of women reporting they had been sexually harassed.

When only the behavior is described. And, when employees were asked, in surveys using probability samples, whether they have experienced one or more specific sex-based behaviors, such as unwanted sexual attention or sexual coercion, the rate of reported harassment rose to approximately 60 percent of women. When they were asked in surveys using convenience samples about such behaviors, the incidence rate rose to 75 percent.

As a result, the EEOC explained, researchers have concluded that many individuals do not label certain forms of unwelcome sexually based behaviors—even if they view them as problematic or offensive—as "sexual harassment."

Sexist or crude behavior. The EEOC went on to talk about the most widely used survey of harassment of women at work, the Sexual Experiences Questionnaire (SEQ). This survey also asks respondents whether they have experienced sexist or crude/offensive behavior. Called "gender harassment" in the SEQ, these are "hostile behaviors that are devoid of sexual interest." Gender harassment can include sexually crude terminology or pornographic displays and sexist comments (like anti-female jokes or comments that women do not belong in management, for example). This behavior is not unwelcome sexual attention; instead, it is intended "to insult and reject women, rather than pull them into a sexual relationship."

When sex-based harassment at work includes this form of gender harassment, almost 60 percent of women report having experienced harassment in surveys using probability samples. The EEOC says that researchers conclude that gender harassment is the most common form of harassment.

Most surveys of sex-based harassment at work focus on harassment experienced by women, the EEOC's report pointed out, but a series of surveys conducted by the Merit Systems Protection Board of federal employees in 1980, 1987, and 1994 also included men. "When respondents were asked whether they had experienced unwanted sexual attention or sexual coercion, 42% of women and 15% of men responded in the affirmative in 1981; as did 42% of women and 14% of men in 1988; and 44% of women and 19% of men in 1994."

Don't miss this! Alexandra, an openly gay assistant project manager in a two-person office, claimed the managing partner, who was also her direct supervisor, forced her to organize marketing events so he could "pimp out" his own wife and his wife's "scantily clad friends" to wealthy customers. Alexandra also accused him of ridiculing and mocking her and telling her that her attire was not feminine enough. She sued the employer for sexual harassment that resulted in a "hostile work environment." Although her employer asked the court to strike her "scandalous" claims because they were not related to her claims of sexual harassment, the court refused to keep the salacious details hidden. Sexual harassment, said the court, includes unwelcome sexual advances, requests for sexual favors, and other verbal or physical conduct of a sexual nature. and there is no requirement that such conduct be directed at the plaintiff/employee. An employee can claim a hostile environment merely for being exposed to an atmosphere where an employer's sexual comments, advances, and actions demonstrate favoritism.

Also, remember that the sensitivities of people differ. What one person may think is funny, someone else may think is inappropriate and unwelcome. Like other forms of workplace harassment, sexual harassment is evaluated by the perception of the victim. In other words, sexual or gender-based conduct in the workplace is unwelcome when an employee *does not solicit or initiate the conduct* and when the employee *reasonably regards the conduct as undesirable and offensive.*

It does not matter whether the person engaging in the conduct would consider the behavior offensive. What matters is whether the individual on the receiving end reasonably finds it offensive.

Guard against "tolerated" behavior

But what if the person on the receiving end acts as if the behavior is acceptable? Is it still sexual harassment? An employee may be reluctant to complain about sexual behavior for a variety of reasons, including fear of job loss, but that does not make the behavior welcome.

Lack of power is often another reason an employee does not report unwelcome behavior. Employees who feel powerless are the most vulnerable to sexual harassment, observes Eric Meyer, noting that traditionally women are more vulnerable to sexual harassment than men. Also included in this group could be employees in lower-paying jobs, younger workers, seasonal employees, immigrants, and migrant workers.

In addition, an employee may be concerned that coworkers will react poorly to a sexual harassment complaint by blaming the employee for encouraging the conduct. And the employee may blame him- or herself. An employee also may be worried about the alleged harasser's reaction if she reports him to management.

Hostile work environment sexual harassment

Hostile environment sexual harassment occurs when unwelcome sexual conduct in the workplace is "severe and pervasive," and unreasonably "interferes with an employee's ability to do his or her job," or "creates an abusive environment." That's the legal standard, but what does this mean in the context of your workplace? It depends.

An isolated incident will rarely be enough to create a hostile environment. Similarly, conduct that is rude or insulting, although inappropriate for the workplace, will probably not rise to the level of sexual harassment. Inappropriate physical conduct or conduct that is intimidating or threatening, however, can add to the severity of the conduct.

Example: During the six weeks that Amy worked for the food and equipment provider, she claimed coworkers called each other offensive names like "Bitchy Ritchie" and "Nipps" and engaged in sexual banter. Amy did not tell anyone, however, that the nicknames or jokes offended her. Amy also claimed that during one out-of-town sales trip, Rick, a male coworker, followed her into her hotel room on the pretense of checking the air conditioner. After dinner, while passing by the hotel swimming pool, he suggested they go skinny-dipping. As they were returning to their rooms, Rick touched Amy's back and told her he would love to watch movies and cuddle. He also suggested they sleep together. She declined and he left. But he later knocked on her door several times.

Amy reported Rick's behavior a week later. An investigation confirmed her allegations and Amy was told she would not have to work with Rick again. In her subsequent lawsuit against the company for sexual harassment, a court found Rick's conduct, while inappropriate, was not severe and pervasive. He did not remain in Amy's room, and did not assault or threaten her. Although his behavior made her uncomfortable, she always felt in control of the situation. Nor was there evidence that this isolated incident altered the conditions of her employment, or created a hostile or *abusive atmosphere. And while the nicknames were also inappropriate, they did not show specific hostility toward women, were used by both men and women, and did not interfere with her work environment.*

What is hostile?

Unfortunately, there is no precise test for determining whether the conduct at issue has created a hostile environment. Courts view the conduct from both a subjective and objective viewpoint. The subjective test examines whether the victim *actually perceived* the conduct to be severe or pervasive enough to create a hostile or abusive environment, while the objective test looks to whether the victim's subjective perception is a *reasonable* one.

Example: *A male coworker sent two text messages to a female employee while she was on vacation, telling her in one to have "wild sex" with her husband, and in the other writing: "You and your husband lay out a wonderful dinner and have wild sex on the table!!! I do think about sex all the time. I just not getting it."*

While inappropriate and unprofessional, this was not severe or pervasive enough to create an environment that a reasonable person would find hostile or abusive. The employee admitted she was able to ignore the first text completely and still considered the male coworker a friend, texting him messages like "You are great and I love working with you." And other than the two text messages, there were no other sexually natured comments or harassing acts. The male coworker never requested sexual favors from the employee nor did he call her any gender-specific epithets at work or off-duty and never grabbed, rubbed, or physically contacted her.

Think back to Jennifer. Once you have investigated Jennifer's allegations, ask yourself whether Roger and Juan's behavior was appropriate. If sexual comments were indeed being made, it's doubtful they belong in the workplace, and appropriate measures should be taken to stop the behavior and prevent it from occurring in the future. This is true *even if* you determine that the conduct does *not* rise to the level of unlawful sexual harassment.

★ Best practices

The best approach in evaluating whether specific behaviors have created a hostile environment is to examine all the circumstances. Key factors HR should consider include:

- The nature of the conduct (physical, verbal, or both);
- The identity of the perpetrator (supervisor, coworker, or nonemployee);
- Whether the conduct was physically threatening or humiliating, or merely an offensive comment;
- The frequency, severity, and pervasiveness of the conduct;
- Whether the conduct was unwelcome (uninvited by and offensive to the victim); and
- Whether the conduct unreasonably interfered with the employee's work performance.

In addition to these factors, there may be other pertinent circumstances to consider in a particular case. Because courts often draw a fine line between what is severe and pervasive and what is not, it is best to have a policy that requires everyone in the workplace to refrain from conduct that reasonably could be considered offensive to others.

Don't miss this! There is no requirement that a person be fired, demoted, lose promotion opportunities, or suffer some other sort of economic or monetary harm in order to sue his or her employer for sexual harassment. Employees are entitled to work in an environment that is free from intimidation, ridicule, or insults based upon their gender. Unwelcome sexual conduct that unreasonably interferes with the ability of a person to work or that creates an intimidating, hostile, or offensive working environment can constitute sexual harassment, regardless of whether a monetary loss occurred.

✔ CHECKLIST: Types of wrongful conduct

Employers can be sued for more than just sexual harassment if the conduct qualifies as wrongful under state "common law" and some state employment discrimination laws. Multimillion-dollar awards have been issued in these types of cases because more damages—both compensatory and punitive—are available than for just sexual harassment claims.

Types of misconduct that can be involved in sexual harassment allegations, which might also result in employer liability under other kinds of legal claims, include:

- ☐ Assault and battery—touching without permission.
- ☐ Intentional infliction of emotional distress—knowing and continual pressure after indications that the behavior was "unwelcome."
- ☐ Loss of consortium—loss of ability to have consensual sex.
- ☐ False imprisonment—being forced to remain in an area and unable to avoid unwelcome advances.
- ☐ Invasion of privacy—unreasonable questioning that intruded into another's personal life.
- ☐ Wrongful discharge—failure to stop harassment, which then forced the victim to quit.

Don't miss this! Just as with other types of workplace communications, sending offensive, degrading sexual comments or jokes or other material, including pornographic or obscene material, over an employer's email system might contribute to the creation of a hostile work environment.

Are compliments wrong?

Can complimenting an employee on his or her appearance be considered sexual harassment? It depends. Although telling an employee on occasion that he or she looks nice will not typically meet the definition of sexual harassment, if the employee is a subordinate and instead of telling him he looks nice, his supervisor constantly tells him he looks really "hot," the result might be different, especially if the employee asks his supervisor to stop, or the "compliments" are also accompanied by unwanted physical contact.

Isolated incidents

Sexual harassment, whether physical, verbal, or both, usually requires a *pattern* of ongoing offensive behavior. Isolated incidents of offensive behavior, such as a male coworker placing his hands on a female employee's shoulder one time, or making a sexual remark about her physical appearance, although inappropriate, generally are not considered sexual harassment.

But like with compliments, it's different when it's the boss. When it is a manager or supervisor who commits sexual or gender-based conduct, the severity factor increases in the eyes of the law. Just one unwelcome touching of an employee's intimate body area by a supervisor may create a hostile environment. Similarly, single incidents of extremely offensive, sexual, verbal conduct by a supervisor could also be deemed sexual harassment.

> **Example:** *Tiffany, a medical records scanner, claimed the CFO of her company made comments that gave her the creeps: he blocked her path in an office hallway; hung around the medical records workroom until Tiffany got permission to lock to door; and finally, on one occasion, he came up behind her, grabbed her waist, and pushed himself against her buttocks. Although a court found that Tiffany's allegations regarding his comments and the hallway blocking were fleeting occurrences that were neither severe nor pervasive, the physical contact incident was a different matter. This, said the court, was a serious charges of uninvited sexual contact that could have created a hostile work environment.*

Participation in the conduct

In some circumstances, a person who has engaged in sexual talk at work can still be a victim of sexual harassment. Remember, when determining whether conduct is sexual harassment, the question is whether or not the conduct is welcome.

Past use of vulgar language or sexual innuendo cannot be used to show that an employee would *never* be offended by sexual comments, or that such conduct is generally welcome. An employee may willingly participate in sexual or gender-based conduct, but then stop. If the employee tells coworkers or others involved that the conduct is no longer welcome, it may be sexual harassment if the conduct continues.

Example: Samara, the only female foreman working in the field for a large construction company, initially engaged in "off-color banter" with her male coworkers, injected sexuality into her communications with them, and even after she was fired texted with or posted on Facebook with some of them, telling them she how much she really enjoyed working with them.

But she later sued the construction company claiming sexual harassment. She said that at first she was just trying to fit in to a male-dominated workforce, but over time she found the repeated sexual comments, innuendos, and overtures troubling. Samara said it took time and a "volume of incidents" for her to more fully understand how bad and demeaning the sexual harassment was. Although the parties hotly disputed the working atmosphere at the company, questions regarding whether the harassing behavior was unwelcome—as well as when she objected to the conduct, and whether she failed to take advantage of the company's sexual harassment policy—would require a lengthy and expensive trial to answer.

Worst case scenario

A metal shop's only female employee, Mary, was subjected to daily harassment by the men in the shop who were unhappy about working with a woman. The men referred to Mary in derogatory terms and subjected her to offensive signs, pictures and graffiti. Mary was also the target of various gender-related pranks, and twice a coworker deliberately exposed himself. Mary complained to her supervisor about the conduct for almost four years before she finally quit and sued the company for sexual harassment.

At trial, the company argued that the harassment was not unwelcome because Mary herself used vulgar language and engaged in "unladylike" behavior. The court rejected this argument since Mary had made it clear through her complaints that the conduct was unwelcome and in light of the fact that she was just one woman against many men. Because there was no evidence that Mary enjoyed or appeared to enjoy the harassment, her participation in the sexual nature of the work environment did not defeat her claim.

Solution. Sexual joking or innuendo—welcome or unwelcome—is inappropriate in the workplace. An employer is inviting trouble if it tolerates such behavior. Comments by one person should not be regarded as an invitation for the rest of the workforce to join in. All comments of a sexual nature observed by HR, managers, or supervisors should be stopped immediately. Employees should be told that such conversations are not appropriate for the workplace.

Remember Jennifer? She told her manager, Seth, that she did not welcome the sexual environment created by Roger and Juan. But it's possible she engaged in sexual banter herself. How should HR respond?

- **Investigate.** First, investigate the situation promptly and take any necessary action to remedy potential harassment. Keep in mind that even if Jennifer did join in some of the sexual talk, her behavior does not necessarily mean she welcomed the sexually charged environment. By complaining to Seth, Jennifer has clearly indicated the conduct is not welcome—even if it was unclear before.
- **Train.** Based on Jennifer's complaint, now would be a good time to re-educate the workforce about harassment. To avoid the perception that they have "welcomed" sexual conduct, employees who no longer want to participate in workplace "sex talk" should be encouraged to firmly tell others that they no longer want to participate.
- **Report.** If the conduct continues or an employee feels uncomfortable confronting his or her coworkers, the employee should be strongly urged to report the behavior to management by following the complaint procedure set forth in the employer's sexual harassment policy. And it should be well understood that if an employee tells a coworker or group of employees that he or she wants the sexual banter to stop—the employees must immediately stop.

Don't miss this! A comment that might seem like good-natured comradery this month is offensive next month if the recipient has become less satisfied with his or her work situation, Sherman and Howard attorney Brooke Colaizzi notes. Effective prevention and remedy of sexual harassment requires up-front diligence from both employers and employees.

Quid pro quo sexual harassment

In the simplest sense, "quid pro quo" means "something for something." Quid pro quo sexual harassment happens when someone with supervisory authority makes unwelcome sexual conduct a condition of the job or the basis for an employment decision—for example, firing an employee because he or she refuses to provide sexual favors.

> **Example:** Amelie reports to Cedric, who has the authority to discharge her. One day, Cedric tells Amelie that he finds her attractive and ask her to join him for dinner. Amelie says "no thanks." A few days later, Cedric again asks Amelie to join him for a dinner date. Amelie turns down his second offer and tells him not to ask her again because she is not interested in him romantically and she is uncomfortable with his repeated requests for a date. Angered by Amelie's rejection, Cedric fires her the next day. Because Cedric terminated Amelie for rejecting his sexual advances, he has engaged in unlawful quid pro quo sexual harassment.

But conditioning continued employment on sexual favors isn't the only way to engage in quid pro quo harassment.

> **Example:** Helen, a female bus driver, was assigned to light duty after injuring herself at work. Over the next few months, her new supervisor, Dennis, repeatedly commented on her appearance, sent her cards and suggestive text messages, and made other unwelcome advances. He also made her go with him when he left the office to run errands. During one of these trips, he placed his hand on her knee and smiled.
>
> When she asked him to stop, he told her she could "have it anyway she wanted," threatened that he could "fix it where there wouldn't be any light duty work available for her" and said she could "stay home and get partial pay." He later asked if she had given any thought to what she was going to do. After a few days of no response, Dennis told her there was no more light duty available, and she would have to take time off.
>
> She ultimately sued her employer, claiming that because she rejected Dennis' advances, she went from working her regular schedule and receiving full pay to receiving two-thirds of her pay under workers' compensation. Because she appeared to suffer a significant change in benefits with a direct economic impact, as a result of Dennis' conduct, their employer might be liable for quid pro quo sexual harassment.

Same-sex and sexual orientation harassment

Same-sex harassment. Sexual harassment does not always involve a man harassing a woman, or a woman harassing a man. It is also unlawful for a man to sexually harass another man and a woman to sexually harass another woman. The issue is whether the harasser is treating the victim in a particular way because of his or her sex.

> **Example:** Not long after Christopher began working for an auto dealer-ship, Stephen, his manager, began groping Christopher's buttocks multiple times a day, touching his shoulders as if to massage him, rubbing his genitals against Christopher's back, and making comments of a sexual nature.
>
> Christopher asked him to stop but Stephen persisted, threatening to have him fired if he complained. Christopher reported the behavior to the company owner. The next day he saw the owner in a hushed conversation with the department manager. About five minutes later, Christopher was fired.
>
> Christopher may be able to successfully sue his employer not only for quid pro quo harassment—his manager conditioned his continued employment on submission to his sexual advances—but also for creating a hostile work environment. Even though it occurred over a short period of time, the manager's conduct may have been sufficiently severe to have interfered with Christopher's work performance and have affected his psychological well-being.

Sexual orientation harassment. Remember that sexual harassment is a form of sex discrimination, and sex discrimination is prohibited by federal law—specifically Title VII of the Civil Rights Act—as well as by state law. Although federal courts had long held that Title VII did not bar discrimination based on a person's sexual *orientation*, things began to change in 2017 when two federal appeals courts decided that discrimination based on a person's sexual orientation is a form of unlawful sex discrimination. In those courts that agree, harassment based on sexual orientation also is unlawful.

In addition, the EEOC also takes the position that Title VII bars any employment discrimination, including harassment, based on gender identity or sexual orientation.

"Gender stereotyping." Even in those courts that still find discrimination based upon sexual orientation is not unlawful sex discrimination under federal law, Title VII's protections against sex discrimination may still bar discrimination based on what is called gender stereotyping—in other words, discriminating against a woman who looks or acts "too masculine" or a man for being "too effeminate."

> **Example:** *A lesbian fast food worker claimed her supervisor sexually harassed her, telling her "I don't like people like you," she needed to "tone down" her attitude to appear more "feminine," and asked her why she lived a "lesbian lifestyle when men liked" her. The supervisor's comments about the employee's sexual identity and "lack of femininity" increased, with the supervisor often making these remarks in front of customers.*
>
> *After she was fired, allegedly for stealing, the employee sued the company for sexual harassment. Although the court explained that discrimination based upon sexual orientation was not actionable under Title VII in the Eleventh Circuit where the lawsuit was filed, it noted that Title VII's protections against sex discrimination do prevent discrimination based on gender stereotyping.*
>
> *But the employee's sexual harassment claim was dismissed by the court anyway. Her supervisor's frequent demeaning comments regarding the employee's sexual identity and lesbian lifestyle were not sufficiently severe to change the employee's conditions of employment from the court's objective perspective. The employee may have been humiliated or degraded by the comments, but the comments themselves were not severe or pervasive, and the employee did not show that the cumulative effect of the supervisor's conduct unreasonably interfered with her job performance.*

Although federal law is still evolving as to whether it protects against harassment based on sexual orientation or gender identity, a number of states and municipalities do have laws that explicitly prohibit sexual orientation discrimination in the workplace. What does this mean for employers? It means employers that do not prohibit harassment based on sexual orientation or gender identity are taking a risk that they may be subject to legal liability if they don't take action to prohibit it. Sexual orientation harassment can be just as harmful to its victims, and the workplace, as sexual harassment, and it should be prohibited by the organization's sexual harassment policy.

Don't miss this! Although a survey released in November 2017 found that a record number of major companies and law firms are advancing vital policies and practices to protect LGBTQ workers, that same month, the U.S. Commission on Civil Rights released a report reflecting the reality that many LGBTQ workers experience prejudice and discrimination in the workplace.

Nonemployee harassment

An employer can also be held responsible for unlawful harassment by third parties in the workplace such as customers, vendors, sales representatives, subcontractors, repair workers, or independent contractors.

Worst case scenario

A former employee of a large warehouse company claimed she was sexually harassed and stalked by a male customer. The customer, she said, stared at her ominously, touched her face, commented on her body, and asked her out multiple times. Although she reported his conduct to management, she claimed the store took no effective action to prevent the harassment and she was forced to obtain a restraining order against him. One manager even angrily rebuffed her and told her to be friendly to the customer after she contacted the police. While the store said it banned the customer from its premises, this was not conveyed to the employee until after she had gone on leave and, according to the employee, until after she had been harassed by him for more than a year.

At trial, attorneys for the EEOC, which brought the case on behalf of the employee, argued that the company knew about the customer's conduct but failed to take appropriate steps to correct the harassment and prevent it from recurring. The conduct created a hostile work environment for the employee in violation of federal law, the EEOC maintained. At the conclusion of a seven-day trial, the jury apparently agreed, awarding the employee $250,000 in compensatory damages.

Off-work conduct

While employment-related harassment usually occurs in the workplace, it can also occur outside of the normal work environment. Typical situations include:

- Employer-sponsored social events—for example, an employer-sponsored holiday party or sporting event.
- Private locations not related to work—for example, after-work drinks at a local bar, restaurant, or hotel.
- Customer locations—for example, during a sales call at a customer's office.
- Cyberspace—for example, while checking email or through text messages or Facebook posts.

Worst case scenario

One night after work, Haydee and a groups of coworkers, including two managers, went to a happy hour at a nearby bar. While there, Arthur, one of her coworkers, tried to feed her food, and asked her where she was going afterward, why she did not let her hair down, and why she seemed uptight. One of the managers witnessed this conduct and reported it to the CEO, who in turn spoke to the HR manager. The HR manager, however, decided not to open a formal investigation because the conduct did not occur at a work event or during work hours.

When Haydee reported the conduct a month later, the HR manager decided to issue a written reprimand to Arthur. Before it was issued, however, Arthur came up behind Haydee, swiped his fingers down her back and, when she tried to get away, grabbed her hand for a couple of seconds. In Haydee's subsequent lawsuit against the company, a court found that a jury would have to decide whether the conduct—which progressed from comments, to touching Haydee with an object (food), to touching her with his body—was severe and pervasive. A jury could also find these incidents were an unwanted invasion of Haydee's physical space of a highly personal and intimidating nature.

And even though the conduct between Haydee and Arthur happened after work hours, off-site, and at a noncompany event, the company might still be held responsible for the alleged harassment. It was reported by a supervisor but no formal action was taken until several weeks later when Haydee filed a separate complaint. As a consequence, Arthur was free to later make comments about the happy hour to Haydee and to escalate his behavior.

And what about social media? Like off-duty social events, social media posts can create particularly challenging situations for employers and can contribute to a hostile work environment, even if the conduct occurs outside of the workplace.

Example: *Emily, a forklift operator, works in a warehouse with all male coworkers. Al, one of the crew members, begins sexually harassing her. After Emily tells him to stop, Al uses his smartphone to post comments on his personal Facebook page, making vulgar comments about Emily's sex life and sexual interest in certain men. The other employees see Al's posts about Emily, and they talk about the posts at work and begin directing epithets at her and simulating sex acts around her. An investigator could find that Al's Facebook posts contributed to a hostile work environment— even though they were written on a personal smartphone and some were written after working hours.*

Workplace romances

Louisa, a line worker at one of your off-site manufacturing plants, calls you on the phone early one morning. She desperately needs some advice concerning a personal situation at work. Louisa reveals that she separated from her husband six months ago and subsequently has become romantically involved with her male supervisor, Chen. Louisa assures you that she and Chen have kept their personal relationship a secret and that there has been no negative effect on their working relationship.

The problem, Louisa explains, is that she has decided to try to make things work with her husband and therefore plans to end her relationship with Chen. Louisa is very concerned about how Chen will take the news and how the break-up will affect her job since Chen is her boss. Currently, your company has no policy that specifically addresses dating in the workplace. How should you handle this situation?

Given the amount of time employees spend at work, it is not surprising that a working relationship may turn into a romantic one. Although a romantic relationship at the workplace is not, by itself, against the law, it can be dangerous—especially if the relationship is between a supervisor and a direct or indirect subordinate. The conduct between the parties can at any time cross the blurry line between a consensual relationship and unlawful sexual harassment.

> **Don't miss this!** A 2018 Vault Office Romance Survey revealed that in a measure of the direct impact of the #MeToo movement, more than 1 in 4 workers indicated that recent allegations of sexual harassment against prominent men have made them less likely to think that romantic relationships between colleagues are acceptable. However, that same survey revealed that 52% of respondents admitted to having had at least one office romance, with "random hookups" being the most common type of relationship.

Is the relationship welcome? Even if an employee consents to the sexual advances of a supervisor, that sexual conduct can still be unwelcome. An employee voluntarily may participate in unwelcome sexual conduct because the employee fears job loss if the sexual advances are rejected. Courts will look at whether the employee acted in a way that would indicate the sexual advances were unwelcome.

Worst case scenario

He said, she said "affair." Prior to being hired as the company's HR Director, Scarlett had only worked as an HR assistant. As part of her duties, Scarlett created an employee handbook for the company, which included a sexual harassment policy. About two years after Scarlett was hired, the company hired Ernst to serve as General Manager. He was also Scarlett's boss.

Almost immediately, according to Scarlett, Ernst made comments to her about sex, exposed himself to her, sent her pictures of himself and requested naked pictures of her, and pressured her into having sex with him. There were approximately 25 sexual encounters between the two, which took place at the office, in Ernst's home, in Scarlett's car, and in hotel rooms. Scarlett claimed she gave in because she felt she had no other option; she attempted to end contact with him, and he told her that she needed to comply with his requests in order to keep her job. According to Ernst, however, the relationship was consensual, Scarlett had initiated it, and they were in love.

Affair revealed. Scarlett ultimately decided to resign. In an attempt to keep the details of her relationship with Ernst private, she denied having a sexual relationship with him, telling her supervisor only that she was having an emotional affair from which she needed to remove herself. But when her husband discovered a text message from Ernst on Scarlett's phone, he contacted the company owner to inform him of the "affair." After Scarlett left the company, Ernst attempted to contact her, allegedly sending her threatening messages. He was terminated after Scarlett contacted the police.

Solution. Pointing to explicit photos Scarlett had sent Ernst, the frequency of their meetings, and her professions of love for him, the company argued that the relationship between Scarlett and Ernst was consensual. She did not end her relationship with Ernst, the company claimed, until she learned that he had made advances to other women in the workplace. Scarlett even admitted that she never explicitly told Ernst she did not want to have sex with him. She claimed, however, that she did not feel she was in the position to do so. As for Scarlett, she said Ernst's affections were unwelcome.

Jury to decide. In a case with similar facts, a court found that whether Ernst's advances and physical interactions with Scarlett were welcome or unwelcome was a difficult issue, and one that would be up to a jury to decide. If Scarlett's claims were true, Ernst's conduct would certainly constitute severe sexual harassment. Either way, the company was facing the prospect of a long, expensive trial.

Intimate behavior at work. A manager and subordinate who openly show affection at work run the risk of offending others and potentially making it more difficult for themselves and others to do their jobs. Even if an isolated kiss in the hallway or a sexually suggestive conversation between a supervisor and subordinate does not create a sexually hostile work environment, it is inappropriate workplace behavior.

The relationship ends. Harassment can follow the break-up of a supervisor-subordinate romance. A spurned supervisor's conduct toward an employee can quickly become unlawful harassment. What was previously welcome sexual behavior may no longer be welcome.

And, if the supervisor takes a negative employment action against the employee as a result of the break-up, the employer will be automatically liable if the victim sues. That there was a prior consensual relationship between the parties will not prevent liability for sexual harassment when post-affair advances by a supervisor are unwelcome.

Preferential treatment of subordinate. Favoritism or preferential treatment based upon the granting of sexual favors can create a hostile work environment for "innocent bystanders"—employees who are offended by the conduct. It does not matter whether the sexual conduct is directed at them or if the favorably treated employees are willing participants. When wide-spread favoritism sends a silent message to employees of one gender that the only way for them to get ahead is to participate in sexual conduct, the employer can be liable for sexual harassment.

Don't miss this! *The EEOC provides these examples of how sexual favoritism may create a hostile work environment:*

- *Sexual favoritism creating hostile work environment: A warden in a county prison engages in sexual affairs with several female correctional officers over a few years. These women were granted prized assignments and promotions. Amber, a correctional officer, is denied a promotion that goes instead to one of the warden's sexual partners, even though Amber is better qualified. Although the warden never directed sexual conduct at Amber, an investigator concludes that Amber was subjected to a hostile work environment based on her sex because she felt pressured to engage in sexual conduct with the warden to obtain desirable assignments and promotions.*
- *Sexual favoritism not creating hostile work environment: Delilah hires Boris to be her personal assistant, and they become romantically involved. Delilah promotes Boris three times in the next 18 months, upsetting Boris's more senior coworkers, both male and female. One of these coworkers, Tammy, files an EEOC charge alleging that she was denied the most recent of these promotions because of her sex. The investigator concludes, however, that Boris was promoted because of his romantic relationship with Delilah, and therefore, Tammy was not denied the promotion because of her gender.*

In the first example above, the warden engaged in widespread favoritism toward those female employees who granted him sexual favors, creating a work environment that was demeaning toward women and produced the perception that women would not be promoted unless they submitted to sexual advances.

In the second example, Delilah's isolated preferential treatment of Boris based on their consensual sexual relationship disadvantaged both male and female employees alike. So while Delilah's behavior may have been totally inappropriate, it did not necessarily create a hostile work environment based on sex.

Take workplace romances seriously

A strong sexual harassment policy that defines and provides examples of supervisor and hostile environment sexual harassment, and one that makes clear that all managerial personnel are subject to it from the CEO or president down the chain, can help to prevent manager-subordinate affairs from crossing the line and becoming unlawful sexual harassment. Employers can set even higher standards by publishing a policy that discourages all sexual activity in the workplace and that disallows any sexual favoritism. Realistically, though, the enforceability of such a policy is problematic.

What about love contracts? Employers may also ban manager-subordinate relationships, but that too can be difficult to enforce and may even infringe on employee privacy rights. What about the use of "love contracts?" Some organizations require employees who are involved in a workplace romance to sign these consensual relationship agreements, in which they admit that they are involved in a consensual romantic relationship and agree to follow certain guidelines regarding appropriate workplace behavior.

Don't miss this! *Love contracts sound good, but in practice, notes attorney Chris Bourgeacq, The Chris Bourgeacq Law Firm, they probably aren't that effective. While a love contract documents a consensual relationship, the relationship can always go south, and [if it does], the contract will not protect against actionable sexual harassment. One alternative would be to simply prohibit dating relationships within the employee's chain of command, since that's where the most exposure to harassment can exist.*

Think back to Louisa and Chen, now that Louisa has informed you that she intends to end their relationship with Chen, her supervisor—and that she is concerned about it. It would be prudent to speak with Chen promptly to let him know that HR is aware of the situation and is determining the best way to proceed. While this may be an awkward conversation, potentially defending a lawsuit over a workplace relationship gone awry will be awkward as well.

In order to ensure that any actions Chen may take as a supervisor concerning Louisa are not perceived as retaliatory, it may be best to end the managerial/reporting relationship as quickly as possible. This too will take tact and sensitivity: If Louisa is to be transferred from Chen's group, for example, make sure that you have her consent and that she does not view the transfer as retaliation, or that her "terms and conditions of employment" are not adversely impacted. You will need to follow up regularly with both Louisa and Chen to ensure no future issues arise.

Now may be the time to consider a policy about workplace relationships, especially those involving a reporting relationship or any significant differential of workplace power and influence (especially those relationships between individuals who are separated by more than one level in the "chain of command"—such as an employee dating his supervisor's boss). At the very least you must consider instructing managers and supervisors to make to make known any intimate relationships with subordinates.

Chapter 3

Employer liability

You just got off the phone with your in-house counsel. An EEOC complaint has been lodged against your organization. Mitzi, a customer service representative who recently resigned claims Al, a coworker, repeatedly made unwanted sexual comments and suggestions to her. She says she complained to her supervisor but he acted like it was no big deal. When she complained again, he joked about it and then told her she needed to "make it work" with Al because he was a top performer. As if that's not enough, Mitzi claims her supervisor then began making sexual comments to her in front of other employees, and even patted her on the butt a couple of times. He also warned her not to say anything to the "higher-ups," as that would make it worse for her. That scared her, she says, because she knew another woman in the office who was "blackballed" after complaining of harassment.

Your in-house counsel said your organization may face "vicarious liability." You're stunned. You knew nothing about this. After all, your organization provides annual anti-harassment training to all employees and has in place a strong anti-harassment policy that includes a detailed complaint procedure with several avenues for reporting sexual harassment. You thought that was all that was required. Can your organization still be legally responsible if harassment occurred?

But that's not even the worst part of your day. Earlier today, you had a conversation with an outside attorney. He is representing Chelsea, a former employee who was recently fired by the HR director for violating the absence policy. You knew that Chelsea had really racked up the absences, but according to Chelsea's attorney, she was actually fired for complaining that the CEO of your organization groped her and forcibly kissed her on two occasions. She alleges the CEO also threatened to take his conduct a step further, stating next time he would "have it all." And she says she's not the only one he's done this to. How can this be happening? What should you do next?

Liability standards

The actions an employer takes, or doesn't take, in reacting to and preventing workplace sexual harassment at every level in the organization can greatly impact an employer's liability for any harassment that does occur. Therefore, employers must be aware of when and why an organization might be held liable for sexual harassment. Liability refers to the point at which a court or federal agency will hold the employer legally responsible for the harassment and require it to pay financial damages to the victim or perhaps take other action.

Employers may be held liable, or responsible, for their own acts of sexual harassment, as well as for sexual harassment committed by supervisors, employees, and nonemployees. Different standards of liability apply depending upon who is held responsible for the conduct.

Alter ego harassment

Starting at the top. An employer may be "strictly" or vicariously liable for workplace sexual harassment committed by someone in the organization that is of sufficiently high rank to be considered the organization's "proxy" or "alter ego." Strict or vicarious liability means the employer will be *automatically* liable—with no defense—even if the victim suffered no "adverse employment action" such as a demotion, loss of benefits, or termination.

Individuals who may be considered a proxy or alter ego of the organization include:

- president;
- owner;
- partner; and
- corporate officer.

Example: *Emily, a clerical worker for a large retail grocer that employed about 600 people, claimed that Lou, one of three senior vice presidents, regularly made comments about how pretty her eyes were, blew her kisses, stared at her breasts, and once kissed her on the forehead. Two days before her wedding, Lou walked into Emily's office, shut the door behind him and then, according to Emily, walked over to her and said he wanted to kiss the bride. He pressed against her and attempted to pull her jaw upward toward him. Emily resisted until he eventually walked out.*

In a case with similar facts, a federal court in Alabama said Emily could take her sexual harassment claims against the company to trial. A jury would decide whether Lou acted as the employer's alter ego, so that his conduct and knowledge were attributed to the company. And if the jury determined that Lou was the company's alter ego, it would not be able to pursue a defense to her sexual harassment claim.

Consider the situation with Chelsea and the CEO. As a high-ranking corporate officer, he could very likely be considered a proxy or alter ego of the company, subjecting it to automatic liability for his actions. While sexual harassment allegations against high-ranking executives may not be anything new, the #MeToo movement certainly brought these allegations to the forefront, forced executives and other powerful individuals out of their jobs, and raised questions about what employers can and should be doing to avoid these potentially catastrophic situations; situations, in which, notes attorney Chris Bourgeacq of The Chris Bourgeacq Law Firm, "there is sometimes an effort to 'save the King' at all costs, which could possibly cloud objective analysis of the claim and possible defenses."

Top executives set the tone

"It is very challenging for an employer when a high-level and valuable employee, upon which the company heavily relies, is the subject of a complaint," Jackson Lewis attorney Stephanie Adler-Paindiris, observes, noting that it is these situations that test the company's "zero tolerance" policy and set the tone for the entire organization.

"It goes without saying that no one in an organization is exempt from sexual harassment laws, nor should any employee accused of harassment be investigated less thoroughly than another because of power, wealth, or performance," notes Sherman and Howard attorney Brooke Colaizzi. "Executives and officers must not only conduct themselves in the same manner as other employees, but by virtue of their position, they are required by law to take action with respect to harassment of which they become aware, and they are responsible for setting the tone and the example for the entire company."

How can employers avoid the challenges that occur when sexual harassment allegations are leveled at the very top of the organization? Employers, Colaizzi suggests, need to ensure that top executives receive the same training as all other employees and are fully aware, not only of the expectations for their own behavior, but also their obligations to address harassment allegations brought to or learned by them.

Don't miss this! *According to Bourgeacq, employers should ensure that executives' contracts have antidiscrimination penalties that forfeit significant compensation and consider limiting reimbursement of defense costs to require successful defense of discrimination complaints. They should also consider having external resources (attorneys or HR professionals) investigate the complaint, and ensure recurring coverage of antidiscrimination harassment training takes place from the top down and is documented.*

The risk is substantial

According to a list that continues to be updated by Vox Media, over 200 powerful and influential individuals—celebrities, politicians, CEOs, and others—have been the subject of sexual harassment or sexual assault allegations in the period between April 2017, when Fox News host Bill O'Reilly resigned, and June 2018. Vox explained that it decided to begin its list with "O'Reilly because his departure from Fox helped set the stage for reports against Harvey Weinstein—which, in turn, helped raise awareness around the #MeToo movement and kick off the reckoning around sexual harassment and assault that continues to this day."

Given the level of power and influence represented by the individuals in this list, encompassing arts and entertainment, media, business and technology, politics, and "other" (including the #ChurchToo movement), employers must realize that the risk of alter ego liability based on the actions of individuals at the top of their organizations may be less remote than they have imagined.

Alter ego liability isn't necessarily limited to situations involving a CEO, although it is somewhat unusual. But it can happen in other contexts.

Worst case scenario

Two women working at a hotel in a central Florida city not known for tourism, one a Filipino housekeeper, the other a white "breakfast bar" worker, were hired and ultimately fired by the hotel's general manager, an Indian man who also held an ownership interest in the business, because they finally resisted his demands for sex. By the time the court heard the hotel's arguments that the case should be dismissed, the general manager had settled with the two women. He was no longer part of the case. Instead, the company that ran the hotel was left holding the bag and tried to defend against the claims, but it looked to the court like there was substantial record evidence that the general manager acted as an "alter ego" of the hotel, holding a high-level position as an owner and general manager, to render the hotel strictly liable for his behavior. The court let the women's claims go forward.

Here is some of the evidence on which the court relied. The women's sexual harassment allegations involved repeated forced sexual encounters, with not only the general manager but also his "friends." The general manager allegedly threatened the housekeeper with the loss of her job, her family, and her husband—and with being sent back to the Philippines—if she did not give him oral sex and have sexual intercourse with him, a "superior" Indian man who told her he was the "big boss," powerful, and he could do anything he wanted, including preventing her from finding another job. She gave in to his sexual demands because she said she could not risk losing her job.

As for the breakfast bar worker, the general manager repeatedly told her that because she was local "white trash," she should give him oral sex or intercourse; if she did not, he threatened her with being fired, but if she gave in, he rewarded her with extra hours. He said white women were lazy, stupid, and garbage, that she was white trash and only good for providing sex to powerful men like him, and that he could do what he wanted because he had power and money. He allegedly told her she would never work again if she complained.

This case is a reminder that sexual harassment often reflects the abuse of power and that alter ego-type liability can crop up in unexpected circumstances.

Supervisor harassment

If the accused harasser is a supervisor in the organization, the employer may, depending on the circumstances, be automatically liable if the victim decides to sue. For this kind of automatic employer liability under federal law, specifically Title VII, a supervisor is defined as someone who has the power to take "tangible employment actions" against the victim.

And if the supervisor's harassment ends in a tangible employment action being taken, the employer will be strictly liable. In other words, it will have no defense if the case goes to court.

Job action taken—automatic liability

A tangible employment action occurs when there is:

- a significant change in an individual's employment status—such as hiring, firing, failing to promote, or reassigning with significantly different responsibilities; or
- a decision causing a significant change in benefits, such as a significant reduction in pay or loss of health benefits.

A direct monetary loss is not necessary in order for conduct to be considered a tangible job action. Rather, the loss of significant job benefits or characteristics of a position—such as the loss of resources necessary for an employee to do his or her job—also may be a tangible job action.

Worst case scenario

Ben works as a supervisor in an insurance company. He makes sexual overtures toward Sonya, a saleswoman. When Sonya rejects his advances, Ben eliminates her private office, dismisses her secretary, causes her files to disappear, and reassigns her work in a manner that results in loss of pay.

Solution. Ben is engaging in inappropriate behavior, and he's putting the organization at extreme risk for liability. In a case with similar facts, a court held the employer strictly liable for the harassment because tangible job actions were taken against the victim. In deciding whether a tangible job action has occurred, don't focus solely on obvious actions—such as a termination or demotion. Although direct economic harm is an important indicator of a tangible adverse employment action, if a supervisor's conduct substantially decreases an employee's earning potential and causes significant disruption in his or her working conditions, a tangible adverse action may be found.

No tangible job action—limited defense

If a supervisor engages in unlawful sexual harassment but the victim does not suffer a tangible employment action, the organization can still be automatically liable, unless it can prove both that:

1. it took reasonable precautions to prevent and promptly correct the harassment; and
2. the victim unreasonably failed to take advantage of any preventive or corrective opportunities provided by the employer to avoid harm.

   Employer's reasonable care. This is critical for employers to understand: What will be considered as taking "reasonable care" to prevent sexual harassment depends on the particular employment circumstances. However, reasonableness generally requires an employer to have in place (1) an anti-harassment policy (2) with an effective complaint procedure that (3) allows an employee to bypass his or her supervisor in reporting the harassment. Also important to the reasonableness inquiry is (4) whether supervisors are effectively trained in preventing workplace harassment and (5) monitoring for EEO compliance.

   Reasonable care also requires (6) immediate and appropriate corrective action by the employer once workplace sexual harassment is known. Remedial measures should be designed to stop the harassment, correct its effects on the employee, and ensure that the harassment does not continue to occur.

> **Don't miss this!** *There are some situations, however, that may make it reasonable for an employee not to complain, including:*
>
> - the employee had reason to believe there was a risk of retaliation;
> - there were obstacles to bringing a complaint; or
> - the complaint mechanism was not effective.

   Risk of retaliation. Here is something else employers must recognize: An employee who reasonably fears retaliation will not be required to use an organization's complaint procedure to report the harassment. To assure employees that such a fear is unreasonable, the employer must clearly communicate and enforce a policy that no employee will be retaliated against for complaining of sexual harassment or assisting in an investigation.

Obstacles to complaints. Some examples of obstacles to bringing a complaint include undue expense by a complaining employee, designating inaccessible officials to accept complaints, or putting requirements on making a complaint that are unnecessarily intimidating or burdensome.

Ineffective complaint mechanism. An employee might reasonably believe that complaining would be ineffective if the organization's complaint procedure requires the employee to first report the harassment to the harassing supervisor. An employee could also reasonably believe reporting harassment would be futile if the employer has a history of failing to stop known harassment.

Think back to the situation involving Mitzi. There was an anti-harassment policy in place but Mitzi never filed a complaint about her supervisor. Doesn't this mean your organization is off the hook? Not necessarily. If Mitzi reasonably believed her supervisor's comments meant he would retaliate against her if she complained, her failure to report his potential harassment might have been reasonable and your organization could still face vicarious liability.

But what about your policy assuring employees there will be no retaliation for reporting sexual harassment? If it's not effectively enforced, it doesn't matter and here Mitzi claimed that another woman was blackballed after complaining. So even if the right policies are in place, failure to enforce them can result in a large jury verdict against the company.

> ### ★ Best practices
>
> #### Employer's actions to prevent and promptly correct harassment avoid trial
>
> Shortly after being promoted to sales and service specialist, Alexis claimed that Jarrett, the banking center manager, began rubbing her shoulders, commenting about going to topless bars, and on one occasion, told her she should work in the lobby area to "get more guys to open up credit cards." Alexis never told Jarrett to stop. She said she was afraid he would get angry or retaliate. Nor did she tell anyone else at the bank about his conduct at the time it was happening.
>
> A few days after Alexis received a warning from Jarrett for repeated tardiness, she took a leave of absence. Upon her return a couple of weeks later, she told an assistant manager Jarrett had been "inappropriate" in

the past, but provided no other details. That same day, she took a second leave of absence. While on leave, she called the bank's HR hotline and reported the harassment.

Two days later, a bank investigator contacted Alexis and then interviewed her, Jarrett, and a number of other employees. Based on the resulting investigation, Jarrett was given a strong verbal warning, told that further inappropriate conduct could result in termination, and required to complete a web-based workplace behavior training course.

Alexis was informed that the bank had taken corrective action against Jarrett and that she would not be subjected to retaliation or other inappropriate conduct upon her return to work. After several extensions of her leave, Alexis resigned, claiming little progress had been made to ensure she felt safe.

Employer did the right thing. Alexis sued the bank for sexual harassment. After first determining that Alexis did not suffer a tangible employment action, the court found the bank acted both to prevent and promptly correct the harassment. The bank maintained policies prohibiting harassment, discrimination, and retaliation, and a policy handbook laid out procedures for reporting harassment, including reporting the conduct to a manger *or* contacting the HR hotline.

Alexis received this handbook when she was hired, as well as additional handbooks throughout her employment, and she admitted she knew the procedure for reporting harassment. The bank also acted promptly after Alexis reported the harassment to the hotline by launching an investigation within two days. As a result of the investigation, Jarrett received a warning and additional training on inappropriate workplace behavior.

Nor did Alexis take advantage of the bank's preventative/corrective opportunities. She did not report her manager's alleged conduct until months after it occurred and when she was already on leave, despite knowledge of the bank's procedure for reporting harassment. Because of its actions, the bank was not liable for sexual harassment under federal law.

The employee's reasonable care. Unless it would be unreasonable to do so, an employee must use the employer's complaint procedure or otherwise bring workplace sexual harassment to the employer's attention. The employee's failure to use a complaint procedure that was communicated and reasonably designed will normally satisfy a court that the employee acted unreasonably.

> **Don't miss this!** It is not necessary to require that an employee reporting sexual harassment complete a particular form, notes Chris Bourgeacq. While there's no reason to prohibit forms, a good intake procedure could require leaving a voicemail, filling out a form, sending an email, or any variety of reporting procedures, including an interview between the alleged victim and HR.

> **Example:** Frances, a waitress, claimed that after months of inappropriate touching and comments, the restaurant owner sexually assaulted her. She immediately left the restaurant and filed a police report. She also sued the employer for sexual harassment.
>
> Her employer argued that it was not liable because it had a sexual harassment policy in place, which Frances had initialed on each page and signed at the end, which required employees to file a complaint of sexual harassment or report the harassment to HR—and Frances never filed a written complaint. But Frances claimed she complained verbally on several occasions.
>
> Because it was unclear what an employee was required to do to file a report, Frances' verbal complaints may have been enough to show she made reasonable use of the reporting procedures. As a result, the employer might not be able to avoid liability for sexual harassment.

Has #MeToo changed the perception of what is reasonable, both for employers and employees?

In light of the #MeToo movement and the realization that sexual harassment is far more common, and more embedded in the workplace, than was commonly understood, there are some signs that the legal interpretation of employer defenses to sexual harassment might change. Self-reflections by those in the employment law community have asked whether employers have focused too much on legal compliance to avoid sexual harassment *liability*, and not enough on sexual harassment *prevention*.

A July 2018 federal appellate court decision sending a sexual harassment case to a jury describes these concerns in a detailed footnote, pointing to:

"a veritable firestorm of allegations of rampant sexual misconduct that has been closeted for years, not reported by the victims. It has come to light, years later, that people in positions of power and celebrity have exploited their authority to make unwanted sexual advances. In many such instances, the harasser wielded control over the harassed individual's employment or work environment. In nearly all of the instances, the victims asserted a plausible fear of serious adverse consequences had they spoken up at the time that the conduct occurred. While the policy underlying [the employer liability affirmative defense] places the onus on the harassed employee to report her harasser, and would fault her for not calling out this conduct so as to prevent it, a jury could conclude that the employee's non-reporting was understandable, perhaps even reasonable. That is, there may be a certain fallacy that underlies the notion that reporting sexual misconduct will end it. Victims do not always view it in this way. Instead, they anticipate negative consequences or fear that the harassers will face no reprimand; thus, more often than not, victims choose not to report the harassment.

"Recent news articles report that studies have shown that not only is sex-based harassment in the workplace pervasive, but also the failure to report is widespread. Nearly one-third of American women have experienced unwanted sexual advances from male coworkers, and nearly a quarter of American women have experienced such advances from men who had influence over the conditions of their employment, according to an ABC News/Washington Post poll from October of 2017. Most all of the women who experienced harassment report that the male harassers faced no consequences. ABC News/Washington Post, Unwanted Sexual Advances: Not Just a Hollywood Story (Oct. 17, 2017).

"Additionally, three out of four women who have been harassed fail to report it. A 2016 Equal Employment Opportunity Commission (EEOC) Select Task Force study found that approximately 75 percent of those who experienced harassment never reported it or filed a complaint, but instead would "avoid the harasser, deny or downplay the gravity of the situation, or attempt to ignore, forget, or endure the behavior." EEOC Select Task Force, Harassment in the Workplace, at v (June 2016). Those employees who faced harassing behavior did not report this experience "because they fear[ed] disbelief of their claim, inaction on their claim, blame, or social or professional retaliation." Id.; see also Stefanie Johnson, et al., Why We Fail to Report Sexual Harassment, Harvard Business Review (Oct. 4, 2016), (women do not report harassment because of retaliation fears, the bystander effect, and male-dominated work environments) (*Minarsky v. Susquehanna County*, 3d Cir., July 3, 2018, Rendell, M.).

The facts of this case are set out in the example below:

Example: A former director for a county made unwanted sexual advances to his part-time secretary for four years; she never reported this. They worked together in an isolated part of the building. Weekly, he attempted to kiss her on the lips and embraced her from behind; he massaged her shoulders and touched her face; he called her at home on her days off and asked personal questions; he sent sexually explicit email from his work email to hers, which she ignored; in fact she asked him to stop. But she feared speaking up to him in any context because he would react and sometimes become "nasty."

The county had a sexual harassment policy that prohibited the type of behavior of which he was accused and encouraged victims to report harassment. The secretary's supervisor, the chief county clerk, knew that the director had engaged in inappropriate behavior with other women; she reprimanded him twice, but the behavior continued. Even the county commissioners knew about his harassing behavior. When the secretary learned that other women had had similar experiences and that a reprimand of the director did not seem to impact his behavior, she felt hopeless. Plus, the director repeatedly warned her not to trust the county commissioners or her supervisor.

It was only after another supervisor overheard the secretary confiding in a friend that the matter was elevated: the secretary was interviewed, the county commissioners were informed, they recommended termination, the director was confronted, admitted the allegations, and was *ultimately fired. But the secretary still sued, and the county defended by arguing it had proved a legally sufficient "affirmative defense:" that as an employer, it exercised "reasonable care to prevent and correct promptly any sexually harassing behavior," and that the employee had "unreasonably failed to take advantage of any preventive or corrective opportunities" or otherwise avoid harm.*

The county argued that its employee handbook, sexual harassment policy, and quick response to the secretary's interview, which surfaced her complaint, satisfied the first requirement—that it exercised reasonable care. It further argued that the secretary waited too long to complain and her delay was unreasonable.

But a federal appeals court wasn't so sure. It asked whether the director's termination was "not so much a reflection of the policy's effectiveness," but instead whether it showed the "County's exasperation, much like the straw that broke the camel's back?" As a result, rather than answer that question, it said a jury should be the judge of whether the county exercised reasonable care.

That court also concluded that a jury should determine whether the secretary unreasonably delayed making a complaint, noting that although courts have "often found that a plaintiff's outright failure to report persistent sexual harassment is unreasonable as a matter of law, particularly when the opportunity to make such complaints exists," it clarified that the "mere failure to report one's harassment is not always unreasonable."

How much time has passed is only one factor, and because sexual harassment depends so much on the particular circumstances, the reasonableness of an employee's actions might well be a jury question. If an employee's "genuinely held, subjective belief of potential retaliation from reporting her harassment appears to be well-founded, and a jury could find that this belief is objectively reasonable," then a jury should make that decision.

Attorney Eric B. Meyer of the FisherBroyles law firm wrote in his The Employer Handbook blog that this case is "the most important employment law decision of 2018." As a result of the court's reasoning that recognized "the chilling effect that misbehaving men in power can have on a victim complaining about harassment," as well as the holes it poked in the employer's defense, Meyer suggested that "employers are staring at more defense costs and bigger overall exposure from the increased risk of a jury trial."

Personal liability

Some courts allow a sexual harassment victim to sue the harasser directly. That means a supervisor who harasses someone may wind up in court defending him- or herself, paying high attorneys' fees, and if found guilty, paying a large sum of money out of his or her own pocket. In some states, the victim may also be able to sue the harasser for claims such as assault and battery, infliction of emotional distress, and invasion of privacy.

Coworker sexual harassment

An employer may also be liable for the actions of coworkers that create a hostile work environment. Unlike sexual harassment by company officials or supervisors, however, employers will not automatically be liable for the harassment. Rather, the EEOC and the courts will ask two basic questions when determining whether an organization is liable for coworker harassment:

- Did the employer know, or should it have known, that harassment was occurring?
- Did the employer take any action to stop the harassment?

Knowledge

An employer's knowledge may come from a complaint made to HR, firsthand observation by a supervisor, or a formal charge of harassment to the EEOC. An employer will also be assumed to know about harassment that is openly practiced in the workplace or is well known among employees. An example might be a nude pin-up calendar and sexually explicit cartoons posted in a common work area.

Failure to report. There is no requirement that a victim actually report workplace harassment. Although that may sound shocking, remember that evidence that the harassing conduct was reported is just one means of establishing employer knowledge. A victim's failure to report the coworker's conduct does not automatically preclude a finding that the employer knew or had reason to know about the alleged harassment.

However, an employer that has distributed an anti-harassment policy that clearly defines the steps an employee must take to report workplace sexual harassment may be deemed not to have notice if a victimized employee fails to report the harassment by taking advantage of the employer's reporting procedure set out in its policy.

Stopping the harassment

Once an employer becomes aware of workplace harassment, it may be found liable for that harassment unless it takes prompt action that is reasonably likely to end the inappropriate conduct. Generally, employers are held to standards that require:

- prompt action—both to investigate and to address the problems created by the harassment;
- measures to stop the harassment;
- measures to correct the effects of the harassment;
- follow-up.

According to the EEOC, the following actions may be considered ways to stop the harassing behavior:

- oral or written warning or reprimand;
- transfer or reassignment;
- demotion;
- reduction of wages;
- suspension;
- discharge;
- training or counseling of harasser to ensure that s/he understands why his or her conduct violated the employer's anti-harassment policy; and
- monitoring of harasser to ensure that harassment stops.

The EEOC cites these examples of how to correct the effects of the harassment:

- restoration of leave taken because of the harassment;
- expungement of negative evaluation(s) that arose from the harassment;
- reinstatement;
- apology by the harasser;
- monitoring how the employee is treated to ensure that he or she is not subjected to retaliation by the harasser or others because of the complaint; and
- correction of any other harm caused by the harassment

Example: *Tamika believed that her coworker, George, was sexually harassing her because he repeatedly asked her to go out on a date with him. Tamika mentioned the situation to a supervisor. The supervisor told HR, and the company investigated thoroughly. Although it was determined that the evidence concerning sexual harassment was inconclusive, HR transferred George to another area where he did not have any contact with Tamika. The company also allowed her to work at home until the transfer was completed. In a case with similar facts, a court found the company promptly stopped the harassing conduct.*

Consider the situation with Mitzi. Should the company have known about the harassment? Although she never filed a formal complaint, she told her supervisor about the coworker's conduct. Not only did he fail to stop it, he joked about it and made sexual comments of his own to Mitzi in front of other employees.

Based on this, a court might very well find the company knew about the harassment and did nothing to stop it, subjecting the company to liability for the coworker's conduct.

Prompt action. If harassment is occurring in the workplace, HR must do more than take remedial action. The action taken must be prompt, effective, and reasonably calculated to end the harassment.

Reassignments. In many cases, employers consider reassigning the alleged harasser and/or victim to different work areas so that they no longer work together. Any such transfer has to be handled cautiously, especially if the victim is to be transferred.

Since federal law prohibits adverse employment actions against an employee who opposes discrimination, the employer must ensure that the new position is substantially equal to the previous position held by the employee and that the employee voluntarily consents to the transfer.

Follow-up. After workplace sexual harassment had occurred and management has taken the appropriate action, HR should follow up with the victim and any witnesses to ensure that the harassment has stopped and that no retaliation is taking place. In addition to protecting the victim from future harassment, this also demonstrates HR's support of the victim for reporting the incident.

Nonemployee harassment

An employer can also be held responsible for unlawful harassment by third parties in the workplace such as customers, sales representatives, repair workers, or independent contractors. More and more courts are holding employers to the same responsibilities as to customer harassment that they are to coworker harassment. As with coworkers, the courts will ask whether the employer knew or should have known about the harassment. If the employer has control over the situation to stop the improper conduct by the third party, immediate corrective action must be taken if feasible.

Worst case scenario

Customer caught by security guard. A security guard for an upscale teen boutique caught a male customer with a camera pointed up a sales associate's skirt, took the customer's cell phone and deleted the pictures and videos, and escorted him out of the store, but failed to provide Tatiana, the sales associate, with the customer's ID information so she could file a police report. She complained to at least three members of management; ultimately, the security guard was disciplined for mishandling the incident. Afterwards, he allegedly urged Tatiana to drop the matter because she was stirring up trouble; he also said he "wouldn't be there to help her" and began touching her inappropriately (physical touching was prohibited) when he "screened" her for loss prevention when she left the store.

Another customer assault. Months later, a second customer grabbed Tatiana's face, put his fingers in her mouth, licked her face, and grabbed her dress before another security guard removed him from the store. The police were not called. Tatiana continued to complain to management, after which she was assigned to work back stock duties, apparently the store's most undesirable assignment. She ultimately quit and sued her employer for sexual harassment.

The store argued neither incident of customer harassment was sufficiently severe or pervasive. But the court allowed her claim to go to trial. It found the second customer incident alone was sufficiently severe to alter the conditions of her employment because it involved direct contact with her intimate body parts—reaching for her face, fingers in her mouth, licking her cheek, and grabbing at her chest and the front of her dress. That alone was sufficiently severe to create a hostile environment, but that wasn't all: In the first incident, a male customer took photographs and videos up her skirt without her knowledge.

What about the security guard's behavior? Then there was the aggressive conduct of the security guard, which the store characterized as "isolated incidents of little to no consequence" that were not sex-based. But the court disagreed about this too. Although not all of the security guard's comments were significant, after the first incident, the security guard approached Tatiana until she was "against the back wall of a cash register," called her a "stupid bitch," got right in her face, and hissed at her that "he would not be there to help her next time." Plus, he arranged to be the one who screened her when she left the store, and Tatiana alleged he reached inside her jacket and touched her sides, her waist, and her hips, even though physically touching employees during screenings was prohibited. Together, those factors satisfied Tatiana's legal burden that the harassment, this time by her coworker, was sufficiently severe or pervasive.

Employer liability for coworker harassment. The retailer argued it couldn't be liable here because "it took effective remedial action immediately upon learning of each customer's misconduct" (Remember it deleted the photos and ejected the first customer, and ejected the second customer). Once it had notice that its employees were being harassed, an employer's remedial obligation is not necessarily satisfied by ejecting an offending customer from the store: "Appropriate corrective action" may also require "proactive steps," said the court.

Preventing future harm. Although ejecting each offending customer was probably necessary to meet the employer's remedial obligations, it was not enough. In fact, there was no evidence of action to prevent future harassment, no employee training, no investigation of either incident, no trespass warning to either customer, and no specific policy on handling customer harassment, despite Tatiana's complaints to multiple management employees. And, while the store claimed it had no advance notice of the customer harassment, even before the first incident management was aware that customers came into the store and tried to look up the skirts of female employees. Because there was a real question as to whether the store failed to take immediate and appropriate corrective action once it knew of the customer's conduct, a jury could impute that conduct to the employer.

The same standards that apply to coworker sexual harassment likely apply to customer harassment. In either case, not every complaint of harassment will result in the employer being held legally responsible.

Example: *An 18-year-old convenience store employee who was fired after a male customer complained that she burned him with a cigarette was unable to show that her employer should be responsible because he had been sexually harassing her. While working the overnight shift at a store where she wasn't usually assigned, the worker was approached by a male customer. He asked her if she had a boyfriend and if she worked there often, and commented about her appearance. He also told her where he lived and worked, mentioned that he had a dashboard camera, and (using a sexually suggestive tone) said that he liked to film things.*

Though two police officers entered the store, she didn't express any concerns to them. After they left, she went outside to smoke a cigarette, while asking a coworker to keep an eye on her since a customer had been "hitting on her." The customer followed her, blocked the store entrance, and said that "his girlfriend calls him when it's raining outside to tell [him] how wet she is, [but that] that's his job." She told him to "back off" and he replied, "What are you going to do about it?" She then extended her cigarette towards him to try to make him move away, but he instead stepped toward her and burned his arm. They both reentered the store, but she did not call the police or report the incident to a supervisor.

The customer returned the next day and reported that she had burned him with a cigarette; the manager reviewed the surveillance tapes and informed the manager of her usual store about the incident. When she reported for her next shift, she was asked if "anything out of the ordinary had happened" while working at the other store. She acknowledged that she had burned a customer with her cigarette, but said she did so to defend herself. She was then fired.

Customer's conduct not severe. *Here, the court found no employer liability for the customer's behavior; the customer's isolated conduct was not sufficiently severe. He never touched or overtly threatened her and though she claimed she felt threatened, she left the store alone to have a cigarette, followed him back into the store, and did not report the incident to the police or to a supervisor. Additionally, liability could not be imputed to the employer because the worker failed to show that it knew of his harassing conduct but failed to take appropriate remedial action. Instead, the employer did not learn about the incident until the customer himself reported it.*

Monitoring manager and supervisors

As part of its anti-harassment program, HR should regularly monitor supervisory employees for compliance with the organization's anti-harassment and EEO policies. HR should also see to it that such compliance is included in formal evaluations. The monitoring function will be particularly important for employers that have supervisors at distant locations without upper management on-site.

One way to regularly monitor supervisory staff for anti-discrimination behavior is to include EEO preventative practices as part of all managers' and supervisors' job responsibilities. To make sure they are carrying out this function, feedback should be requested in the same way as it is with any other supervisory responsibilities. And if a manager fails to report harassing, discriminatory, or inappropriate conduct, appropriate disciplinary action should be taken.

✔ CHECKLIST

The following recommendations, provided by attorney Chris Bourgeacq, are examples of effective processes he has seen for handling sexual harassment complaints:

☐ Promptly acknowledge the complaint and assure the employee that it will be taken seriously and investigated as soon as possible.

☐ Remind the complainant and witnesses interviewed to keep the investigation confidential while it is pending. This is especially true in situations where the complainant or witnesses might fear retaliation from the accused harasser.

☐ Be sure to interview the complainant. And, of course, interview the accused harasser.

☐ Be consistent in the approach toward similar investigative findings. Firing a low-level manager, but not the senior VP, for the same conduct is not acceptable and clearly sends a wrong message to those aware of the misconduct.

☐ Strict application of a zero tolerance policy is an easy approach to follow, but may not apply in every case. It could also result in unfair results in close cases. Better to reserve discretion in your policy and try to be as consistent as possible in resolving complaints.

☐ Be discreet in releasing results of the investigation. Have a closure meeting with the accuser. However, the accuser is not entitled to know all the details of your investigation, nor is he or she allowed to know exactly what corrective action, if any, took place with the alleged harasser.

Chapter 4

Policy creation and communication

Rafael, an employee in your organization, recently handed in his resignation. You just met with him for his exit interview, and when you asked why he decided to resign, he responded, "I felt I had no other choice." After further prompting, Rafael reluctantly tells you that almost immediately after he was hired, his supervisor, Brenda, started sexually harassing him. When he told her to stop, she got mad, and began criticizing his work and writing him up for minor things, he said sadly. Although he claimed he told Gordon, a manager in a different department, about Brenda's actions, Gordon just laughed and told him he had to report Brenda's conduct up his own "chain of command." Gordon also warned him to be careful because, he whispered, Brenda doesn't like to be crossed and has a reputation for "getting even."

You've just looked at your sexual harassment policy, which has not been updated in a long time. Although the policy states that the company will not tolerate sexual harassment, it does not specifically prohibit retaliation. It also advises employees to report harassment to their immediate supervisor. You know you need to revise the policy to ensure that a situation like this does not happen again, but what kind of changes should you make? And what are you going to do about Rafael—or more importantly, Brenda?

Why have a policy?

Well before the #MeToo movement, most companies maintained sexual harassment policies and provided some sort of sexual harassment training. Yet sexual harassment in the workplace obviously continues to be a problem; a significant problem, in fact. Then why have a sexual harassment policy? An organization that does not establish and distribute a clear policy—and does not provide a reasonable avenue for victims to complain to someone with authority to investigate and remedy the problem—may be held liable for unlawful harassment *regardless* of whether it knew about the conduct.

So what can an employer do to improve the effectiveness of its policy?

The first step may be to look at some of the most significant barriers to having an *effective* policy. "Policies cannot simply sit in a handbook," stresses Jackson Lewis attorney Stephanie A. Paindiris. Instead, Paindiris suggests that:

- Sexual harassment policies must be modeled from the top;
- All employees must be trained on the policies;
- Managers and leaders must repeatedly communicate the message of the policies; and
- Employers must monitor the policies to ensure they are working as intended to prevent harassment.

Other significant barriers include failing to enforce the policy, insufficient training, and employer complacency.

"Employers need to have a feel for their culture and environment before an allegation is made," observes Sherman and Howard attorney Brooke Colaizzi. "They need to be proactive in identifying problems, tensions, or dissatisfactions that could contribute to sexual harassment allegations."

> **Don't miss this!** An employer was ordered to pay $70,000 and provide other relief to settle allegations that a store manager subjected a female sales associate to unwanted sexually laced comments, text messages, and gestures. Even though other female employees had previously complained about the same manager, the harassment continued, according to the EEOC, which investigated the sales associate's complaint. In fact, the employer allegedly continued to employ the manager for several months after her initial complaint.

- In addition to the monetary relief, an 18-month consent decree resolving the case required: mandatory sexual harassment training, with "civility and bystander intervention training," for all employees including the district manager, store manager, and assistant store manager;
- annual training for the store manager, district manager, regional directors, and HR managers;
- notification to the EEOC of future sexual harassment complaints; and
- annual reporting of sexual harassment complaints and training.

Observed an EEOC trial attorney, "having an anti-harassment policy that looks good on paper does not satisfy federal prohibitions against sexual harassment in the workplace … employers must also enforce it. An unenforced anti-harassment policy is tantamount to having no policy at all."

Key provisions

There is no doubt that a comprehensive sexual harassment policy is an essential part of your effort to prevent workplace sexual harassment. But what should be in the policy? The EEOC suggests that a comprehensive harassment policy include:

- A statement that the policy applies to employees at every level of the organization, as well as to applicants, clients, customers, and other relevant individuals;
- An unequivocal statement that harassment based on a legally protected characteristic is prohibited;
- An easy to understand description of prohibited conduct, including examples;
- A description of any processes for employees to informally share or obtain information about sexual harassment without filing a complaint;
- A description of the organization's sexual harassment complaint system, including multiple (if possible), easily accessible reporting avenues;
- A statement that employees are encouraged to report conduct that they believe may be prohibited sexual harassment (or that, if left unchecked, may rise to the level of prohibited harassment), even if they are not sure that the conduct violates the policy;
- A statement that the employer will provide a prompt, impartial, and thorough investigation;
- A statement that the identity of individuals who report harassment, alleged victims, witnesses, and alleged harassers will be kept confidential

to the extent possible and permitted by law, consistent with a thorough and impartial investigation;

- A statement that employees are encouraged to respond to questions or to otherwise participate in investigations regarding alleged harassment;
- A statement that information obtained during an investigation will be kept confidential to the extent consistent with a thorough and impartial investigation and permitted by law;
- An assurance that the organization will take immediate and proportionate corrective action if it determines that harassment has occurred; and
- An unequivocal statement that retaliation is prohibited, and that individuals who report harassing conduct, participate in investigations, or take any other actions protected under federal employment discrimination laws will not be subjected to retaliation.

In addition, HR should ensure that the policy is written in language that is easy to understand. If you have employees that speak languages other than English, make sure your policy is translated into those languages as well.

Define sexual harassment

Because it is so often misunderstood, it is a good idea to provide a working definition of sexual harassment. Your policy should also state that the victim, as well as the harasser, may be a woman or a man, and the victim does not have to be of the opposite sex as the harasser. Make clear in your policy that no employee should be subject to conduct that is sexual in nature or that shows hostility to the employee because of the employee's gender or gender identity.

In fact, it is a good idea to spell out in your policy that this includes harassment on the basis of an employee's real or perceived sexual orientation (lesbian, gay, bisexual, asexual, pansexual, or straight), or their gender identity. This encompasses harassment because of others' perception of an employee's sexual orientation or gender identity, whether that perception is correct or not. Whether or not federal or state law yet requires protections for individuals on the basis of sexual orientation or gender identity, many state laws do, and encompassing these characteristics within your organization's definition of sexual harassment is consistent with your policy of respect for all others.

For example, state that:

Sexual harassment does not refer to occasional compliments of a socially acceptable nature. It refers to unwelcome behavior of a sexual nature that is personally offensive, that makes a person feel humiliated or intimidated, and that interferes with work effectiveness. Both men and women can be victims of sexual harassment. A victim can be of the same sex as the harasser. The harasser can be a supervisor, coworker, other [Organization] employee, or a nonemployee who has a business relationship with [Organization].

Sexual harassment includes, but is not limited to, making sexual advances or requests for sexual favors, as well as other forms of verbal or physical conduct that show hostility toward an employee because of the employee's sex, sexual orientation, or gender identity, where either:

- *submission to the conduct is an explicit or implicit condition of employment; or*
- *submission to or rejection of the conduct is used as a basis for employment decisions; or*
- *the conduct has the purpose or effect of substantially interfering with work performance or creates an intimidating or offensive work environment.*

Prohibited sexual harassment also includes conduct that takes place outside of [Organization] premises, including at social events, training sessions, and business trips.

You can also help employees understand the types of behavior that are inappropriate for the workplace by including examples of potentially harassing conduct.

✔ CHECKLIST: Examples of sexually harassing conduct

Sexually harassing conduct includes both verbal and physical conduct. Examples of inappropriate conduct or behavior include, but are not limited to:

☐ Asking unwelcome questions or making unwelcome comments about another person's sexual activities, dating, personal or intimate relationships, or appearance.

☐ Engaging in unwanted and repeated invitations for off-duty socializing, dates, or physical intimacy.

☐ Engaging in sexual pranks, or repeated sexual teasing, bullying, jokes, or innuendo, in person, by phone, through email, through texting, or through any other forms of social media.

☐ Emailing or texting sexually explicit pictures or other material.

- [ ] Displaying objects or pictures that are sexually suggestive or that demean or show hostility to a person because of the person's sex, sexual orientation, or gender identity.
- [ ] Engaging in inappropriate touching or unwelcome physical conduct including hugging, kissing, patting, massaging, pinching, or fondling.
- [ ] Threatening adverse employment actions or promising rewards in exchange for sexual favors.
- [ ] Sexual assault, threatened or actual.

Respect is key. To make sure that workers don't get into a guessing game over what is technically unlawful behavior and what is not—which can easily happen—insist that employees, and individuals with whom the organization has a business relationship, treat each other with respect. Explain that behavior that does not rise to the level of unlawful sexual harassment, but that a reasonable person would still find *offensive and inappropriate for the workplace*, violates the organization's policy against inappropriate behavior. Advise workers to use common sense in their interactions with coworkers, managers, and persons outside the organization.

Complaint procedure

Just as important as the employer's stance against workplace sexual harassment is the mechanism it has in place for ensuring that such behavior does not occur. Workers must know how to bring their concerns about workplace sexual harassment to someone's attention.

> **Don't miss this!** According to the Society for Human Resource Management research results released in January 2018, 94 percent of surveyed HR professionals said their organizations have anti-harassment policies. Yet 22 percent of non-management employees did not know for sure that these policies existed.

Why is a complaint procedure important? How are employees going to know how to respond if their organization has no specific procedures for dealing with harassment? If no effective complaint procedure is in place, it is reasonable for employees to believe that harassment will be ignored, tolerated, or even condoned by management. That's the first reason a complaint procedure is important.

Additionally, when a supervisor engages in sexual or other unlawful harassment, the employer likely will be automatically liable if no policy against harassment has been established and if there is no system to allow victims to complain to someone with authority to investigate and remedy the problem. Even if the harasser is a coworker or nonemployee, the employer may still be liable because it should have known of the harassment, yet did not know, only because the employee had no effective means to report it.

On the other hand, an effective complaint procedure that encourages employees to complain about sexual harassment puts the employer in a stronger position to defend against a sexual harassment claim. In the case of harassment by a manager or supervisor, the employer may be able to escape otherwise automatic liability. And, if a complaining employee has no legitimate reason for failing to use the complaint procedure, his or her credibility may be damaged. It is also more difficult to claim that harassment forced an employee to quit his or her job if the employee did not use an effective complaint procedure before quitting.

> **Don't miss this!** *A complaint procedure will be deemed ineffective if the persons designated to receive complaints are all close friends of the harasser, or require a complaint to be made to the harasser, and there are no alternative avenues for complaining. An employee's failure to complain might be considered reasonable if the employee knows the employer failed to take appropriate corrective action in response to prior complaints filed by the employee or by coworkers. Other reasons an employee's failure to use the complaint procedure may be considered reasonable include unnecessary obstacles to filing complaints, inaccessible points of contact for making complaints, or unnecessarily intimidating or burdensome requirements.*

Remember Rafael, who was told he had to report his supervisor's alleged harassment "up his own chain of command?" If it turns out that Rafael was a victim of sexual harassment, your organization could have trouble claiming he should have complained about the conduct if he indeed was supposed to report his harasser's conduct to the harasser herself, and there was no effective complaint procedure in place that included alternative avenues for complaining.

And what about his attempted complaint to Gordon? Your policy should stress that managers have an obligation to report *any* harassment of which they become aware by any means—their own observations, the observations of others, and because they were told (or overheard) a complaint.

How can HR establish an effective reporting mechanism? For one, make sure the policy urges employees to come forward and report incidents of improper workplace behavior as soon as they happen. Next, outline a procedure for employees to make complaints about harassment. Make sure the avenues of complaint are accessible. For example, if you have a 24-hour workforce, make sure complaints can be brought 24 hours a day. If you have a hotline, be sure to publicize it: Put it in written memos, post it in facilities, put it on the organization's employee-facing website, put it in handbooks, include it in training.

Don't miss this! An effective harassment complaint system, says the EEOC, welcomes questions, concerns, and complaints; encourages employees to report potentially problematic conduct early; treats alleged victims, complainants, witnesses, alleged harassers, and others with respect; operates promptly, thoroughly, and impartially; and imposes appropriate consequences for harassment or related misconduct, such as retaliation.

★ Best practices

Employee hotlines

A robust hotline offering can help provide evidence that an employer reasonably tried to prevent and promptly correct the harassing behavior; and, if the employee did not use the hotline, that the employee unreasonably failed to take advantage of any preventive or corrective opportunities provided by the employer. Red Flag Reporting, an organization that provides a hotline reporting service, has identified a number of best practices in implementing a reporting hotline.

- Identify which features of a hotline are important to your organization; you may not need advanced functionality like case management.
- Determine whether to operate the hotline internally (for example, a voicemail box or an email address) or use a third party.
- Determine how you will address anonymity. Many hotline users choose to report anonymously for fear of being identified, a concern that may create distrust in using an internal hotline. Don't record where calls originate from or track IP addresses. Anonymity is a key feature that makes hotlines effective.

- Provide numerous reporting mechanisms: more is better. Provide a website, a toll-free number, an email address, and a mailing address; even a fax number. Reporting via a website has some advantages, because users are less afraid their voices will be recognized. Some users are more able to think through the details being provided in such a format, especially if guided questions are provided, as opposed to being presented only with an empty data box to fill in.
- Consider at what point in the process an employee will reach a live person. Having live contacts can guide hotline users, who are often traumatized, into making a more coherent and complete report. Automated and recorded calls utilizing voicemail may discourage individuals who fear the loss of anonymity. Also, unguided questioning may result in incomplete information. Consider making a live person reachable 24/7 given that employees may wait to contact a hotline until after working hours.
- Make certain employees are aware of the hotline and that they trust it. It also helps to stress that subjects of hotline reports are "innocent until proven guilty," as well as to stress that anyone who files a hotline report in good faith will be protected from retaliation. Provide information about the hotline with training; post notices about the hotline, and include periodic reminders in employee communications. Create desktop links to the hotline, for example.
- Management needs to accept the hotline too. There is a common fear that the hotline will be abused, but there is little evidence to support that fear. Implementing a hotline instead sends a clear message to the organization that "acting in an ethical manner counts."
- Demonstrate support from executive-level management. Have an executive-level member of management reveal the program to employees. Managers and supervisors should then reinforce the message. Stress that the hotline's purpose is to protect employees— and the organization—not to create a "big brother" environment.
- Always identify at least two people to be notified when a hotline report is received.

Be sure to provide several avenues for an employee to report harassment so that the employee can bypass his or her supervisor, who might be the alleged harasser. If possible, it is a good idea to designate both males and females as persons to report to because an employee might feel more comfortable reporting harassing behavior to someone of the same sex. Also include the name and phone number/email address of the department that maintains and monitors the policy, and identify who is responsible for responding to questions and concerns.

As the situation with Rafael's attempted report to Gordon illustrates, it is a good idea to state in the policy that supervisory personnel are required to immediately report suspected harassment. Supervisors are considered agents of the organization and as such should understand their responsibility for protecting it and the employees who work for it. In fact, stress that a manager or supervisor's failure to report harassment will result in appropriate discipline, which may even include termination.

Don't miss this! *The EEOC recommends that an effective harassment complaint system:*

- Is fully resourced, enabling the organization to respond promptly, thoroughly, and effectively to complaints;
- Is translated into all languages commonly used by employees;
- Provides multiple avenues of complaint, if possible;
- Provides prompt, thorough, and neutral investigations;
- Protects the privacy of alleged victims, individuals who report harassment, witnesses, alleged harassers, and other relevant individuals to the greatest extent possible (but does not guarantee confidentiality), consistent with a thorough and impartial investigation and with relevant legal requirements;
- Includes processes to determine whether alleged victims, individuals who report harassment, witnesses, and other relevant individuals are subjected to retaliation, and imposes sanctions on individuals responsible for retaliation;
- Includes processes to ensure that alleged harassers are not prematurely presumed guilty or prematurely disciplined for harassment; and
- Includes processes to convey the resolution of the complaint to the complainant and the alleged harasser and also, where appropriate, the preventative and corrective action taken as a result.

Who receives harassment complaints? You know that HR needs to designate and train several persons to receive complaints of harassment, but who should be chosen? These persons may include supervisory or managerial personnel, the head of human resources, the organization's EEO officer, or someone else the organization designates. Just remember that there must *always* be an alternative path for reporting incidents of sexual harassment in case the alleged harasser is the person to whom the complaint would otherwise be made.

✔ CHECKLIST: Selecting persons to receive complaints

When deciding who should receive complaints, there are several considerations:

☐ Are the designated representatives reasonably available when employees are working, including evening and weekend shifts?

☐ Is each representative someone to whom employees would feel comfortable bringing a complaint?

☐ Is each representative sufficiently trained to respond effectively to complaints of workplace harassment?

☐ Is the representative able to maintain privacy and confidentiality to the extent the law permits it?

☐ Does each representative have the authority and resources needed to initiate an investigation and participate in the resolution of complaints?

☐ Where an organization has multiple locations, but does not maintain an HR person at each site, is there an appropriate officer or management employee available at every site?

★ Best practices

Sample complaint procedure provision

Any employee who believes he or she has been the target of sexual harassment is *encouraged* to inform the offending person orally or in writing that the conduct is unwelcome and offensive and must stop.

The employee should also report the conduct to the employee's immediate supervisor or to Human Resources, which has responsibility for maintaining and monitoring this policy. Employees may also report sexual harassment or violations of the organization's respect rule to any other member of [Organization] management or through [Organization's] 24-hour hotline at [hotline phone number/email].

All leaders must immediately inform Human Resources of any complaints received. A leader who has not received a complaint but who suspects conduct that might violate this policy must immediately inform Human Resources, regardless of how the leader became aware of the conduct.

All allegations of sexual harassment will be quickly investigated. To the extent possible, the complaining individual's confidentiality and the confidentiality of any witnesses and the alleged harasser will be protected against unnecessary disclosure. When the investigation is completed, affected employees will be informed of the outcome of that investigation as necessary.

Don't miss this! Small organizations can be confronted by unique issues. For example, what if the HR function is directed by a relative of the accused harasser? Suggests attorney Chris Bourgeacq, of The Chris Bourgeacq Law Firm, "If there's a reason to suspect the HR relative will be nonresponsive, engage other leaders in the business—e.g., the general counsel, COO, or even the board of directors or an individual director."

Protection from retaliation

HR must make sure that all communications regarding the organization's sexual harassment policy stress that employees will not be retaliated against for bringing a complaint of sexual harassment. Nor will there be any retaliation for providing support as a witness in a harassment investigation.

State in your policy that no one reporting inappropriate conduct will be disciplined or retaliated against, even if a report made in good faith is later determined to be unfounded.

Include in your prohibition against retaliation protection for any employees who assist in investigating complaints of improper conduct. Make clear that any employees who engage in retaliatory conduct are subject to discipline up to and including termination.

Don't miss this! Federal law prohibits retaliation against an employee because he or she has opposed discriminatory practices by making a complaint or participating in an investigation. To reduce the risk of retaliation claims, employers should take care before making any employment decision that could be perceived as having a negative effect on someone who has complained about sexual harassment or participated in the investigation of a harassment complaint. If disciplinary action against an employee who has reported harassment or participated in an investigation is warranted for unrelated reasons, it might be wise to consult legal counsel before taking action.

Think back to Rafael, who was warned—by one of your managers!—to be careful about reporting his supervisor's alleged harassment because she didn't like to be crossed. Rafael needed reassurances from the organization that his complaint would be taken seriously and that he would be protected from retaliation. Because he didn't get such reassurances, he chose to remain silent and find another job. He also could have chosen to bring his complaint to an outside agency, like the EEOC, and the organization could have not only faced losing a valuable employee, but also the expense and disruption of an agency investigation and potential lawsuit.

★ Best practices

Sample complaint procedure provision

[Organization] will not permit any employment-based retaliation against anyone who brings a complaint of sexual harassment or who speaks as a witness in the investigation of a complaint of sexual harassment. Any person found to have retaliated against another individual for reporting sexual harassment, participating in an investigation, or taking any other actions protected under federal employment discrimination laws will be subject to appropriate disciplinary action, up to and including termination.

Prompt investigation

A statement in the sexual harassment policy about the investigation process is a good idea. For example, HR may choose to say that once a complaint of workplace harassment is made and the employer is aware of the problem, an immediate internal investigation will be conducted according to the employer's policy.

Communicate that the goal of the investigation will be to gather all facts so that management can determine whether inappropriate conduct has occurred. Assure that the facts will be kept confidential under a strict "need to know" basis as much as possible.

HR may also want to explain what will happen once the investigation is complete. It is probably not a good idea to promise disclosure of full details. Rather, state that the parties will be informed of the results and if corrective action was taken. Caution that the person who made the complaint usually will not be told about the particulars of the disciplinary actions being taken, other than that the employer has acted appropriately. Encourage workers who are involved in a sexual harassment investigation to immediately let management know if there are any further problems.

> **Don't miss this!** *The #MeToo movement has resulted in sexual harassment allegations now surfacing involving events that may have occurred months, years, and even decades earlier. What should an employer do if it learns, through a formal complaint or otherwise, that sexually harassing behavior may have occurred a long time ago but was never reported? Many experts suggest treating every complaint, even "stale" complaints, seriously, and opening an investigation even though the investigation may face issues with unavailable witnesses, uncertain memories, and missing evidence.*

Confidentiality

Don't promise what you can't deliver: It is best to assure confidentiality without promising absolute secrecy. Assure anyone who complains of harassment only that all complaints will be handled as confidentially as possible. State that once an investigation has begun, the facts will be kept under a strict "need to know" basis as much as possible. Advise participants that all individuals involved in the harassment—including the complainant, the accused, and witnesses—will be asked to keep investigatory discussions confidential.

✔ CHECKLIST: Persons with a "need to know"

People who would likely need to be apprised about the facts of a sexual harassment investigation include:

☐ persons investigating the complaint;
☐ the person accused of harassment;
☐ witnesses;
☐ persons involved in making decisions based on the outcome of the investigation; and
☐ any other management-level persons who have a legitimate need to know.

Disciplining the offender

Many experts recommend that the sexual harassment policy include a statement of what the organization will do if, following an investigation, harassment is found to have occurred. This means setting forth the disciplinary measures that may be taken against anyone who is found to have violated the policy.

For example, the policy may state that a supervisor or employee who is found responsible for harassment will be disciplined, and that the degree of the discipline will reflect the severity of the conduct and who had engaged in the conduct. State that discipline can include oral or written warnings, reprimands, demotion, suspension, and probation.

If the conduct is very offensive or if the victim's ability to perform is significantly impaired, explain that discharge may be the only alternative. Also, be clear that if the harasser is a supervisor, the most severe penalty— discharge—may be necessary. HR may also want to include a statement that all actions the organization takes as a result of a policy violation will be consistent and timely.

★ **Best practices**

Zero tolerance policies

According to a study co-authored by a Florida International University professor entitled "How Organizational Policies Influence Bystander Likelihood of Reporting Moderate and Severe Sexual Harassment at Work," employees are more likely to report sexual harassment they witness at work when there is a zero-tolerance policy in place.

Findings from the study show companies where zero-tolerance policies are a top priority are particularly effective in increasing the *reporting* of the most common forms of sexual harassment, whether moderate or severe, including sexually suggestive remarks that create a hostile work environment. Results also show a zero-tolerance organizational policy can increase the likelihood that more severe harassment, including quid pro quo, would be reported by employee bystanders.

According to the study, a standard policy statement saying "we are an equal opportunity organization and subscribe to federal and state laws which forbid discrimination and harassment" is not as effective as a zero-tolerance policy that provides a clear framework for interpreting and acting on what someone may witness or experience.

Recommended steps. The researchers recommend these steps to implement an effective zero-tolerance policy:

1. **Look at your policy:** Does your organization have a zero-tolerance policy that explicitly prohibits both moderate and severe sexual harassment? Does leadership adhere to the policy and frequently ensure it is understood by all members of the organization? Does it rely too heavily on victim reporting? Optimal policies bring *all* employees into the circle and encourage a culture that does not tolerate harassment.

2. **Encourage diversity:** Organizations and industries that are numerically male-dominated and have less gender diversity may be more likely to experience sexual harassment in the workplace and substantially more likely to experience it if the policies and culture are not in place. Diversity in leadership is also important.

3. **Follow-through:** Leaders need to set the tone for the organization and be explicit in their expectations. When harassment is reported, perpetrators should be held accountable.

Communicating the policy

Obviously, the best policy will do no good if nobody knows about it. Therefore, it is just as important that HR communicates the policy as it is that HR creates it.

Don't miss this! Lack of dissemination and enforcement is a significant barrier to the effectiveness of sexual harassment policies, notes attorney Chris Bourgeacq. "Some employers have great policies on their face but do very little to cover them with employees," he explained. Just handing out a sexual harassment policy with other volumes of paper during a new hire orientation/onboarding process is not enough.

Distribute and post

The policy should be distributed to all new employees during the onboarding process. It is best that HR also redistribute the policy on a regular basis—perhaps annually or more frequently if external circumstances suggest it may be appropriate, such as the existence of new harassment reports garnering extensive media coverage. This serves as a way to remind employees periodically of the organization's position against sexual harassment.

There are various methods HR can use to remind employees of the sexual harassment policy, for example, from the annual required online policy review that many organizations undertake, to periodic reminders during the performance review process, to distributing a paper copy of the policy annually in the envelope with an employee's paycheck.

HR should also post the policy in all the organization's locations, where possible, and incorporate it into employee handbooks. If the workforce is online, of course the policy should be posted electronically as well. But regardless of how many options employees are given to access the policy, HR must routinely verify that it is current, and make any changes that changes in the law or circumstances require.

Don't miss this! Employers that hire workers who are unfamiliar with English must ensure that the policy is correctly and accurately translated into the required language or languages. The translated policy should be carefully edited for grammatical correctness and readability for your non-English-speaking workforce. If at all possible, it is desirable to have bilingual personnel available to help ensure optimal communication of the policy.

★ Best practices

Sample provision

Communication of policy. [Organization]'s sexual harassment policy is included in the [Organization] handbook, posted on the [Organization] intranet, and posted in several conspicuous locations in the workplace. You will also receive a copy of [Organization's] sexual harassment policy when you begin working for [Organization]. If at any time you would like another copy of that policy, please contact _____ . If [Organization] should amend or modify its sexual harassment policy, each employee will receive an individual copy of the amended or modified policy.

Train

Train all employees and supervisory staff on the policy to make sure that they understand their rights and responsibilities. Discuss and explain the policy during group meetings. Managers and supervisors should receive specific training to enforce the policy and to be sensitive to improper conduct. Further, supervisory staff should be trained to take appropriate actions. Keep records of attendance at training sessions.

> **Don't miss this!** *Insufficient training can prevent even the best sexual harassment policy from being effective. "No policy is the world provides a good practical picture of what is and is not 'sexual harassment,'" notes attorney Brooke Colaizzi. "Training needs to include plenty of real-life examples, case studies, and role playing so that employees really know what sexual harassment is."*

★ Best practices

Sample training provision

All [Organization] management personnel will participate in sexual harassment awareness and prevention training. In addition, all employees will participate in a workshop about sexual harassment upon beginning work at [Organization] and, at least _____ while you remain an [Organization] employee.

Get acknowledgement

It is very important that employers document their efforts to prevent and eliminate harassment in the workplace. To that end, HR should require workers to sign a form (paper or electronic) acknowledging that they have received and read the organization's sexual harassment policy and promising that they will abide by the rules contained in it. That way, if there is ever a dispute concerning whether an employee knew about the policy and complaint procedure, HR can access the acknowledgment form.

★ Best practices

ABA adopts resolution to combat sexual harassment

In its first meeting since the #MeToo movement swept the country, the American Bar Association's House of Delegates in early 2018 adopted a resolution urging all employers to adopt and enforce policies and procedures that prohibit, prevent, and promptly redress harassment based on sex. The resolution expands ABA policy and establishes new components for enforcing policies and procedures aimed at preventing harassment and retaliation, including:

- disseminating a "clear statement" to all employees and management that such harassment will not be tolerated;
- a confirmation that the policy applies to conduct by directors, officers, management at all levels, supervisors, employees, and third parties, at or in connection with any work-related function, no matter where that conduct occurs;
- alternative methods for reporting policy violations, including a method that sidesteps any accused individuals, and at least one confidential anonymous reporting method, such as a hotline;
- communicating the process for reporting harassment complaints to a governmental agency, and the potential relief therefrom;
- investigating complaints in "a prompt, competent, fair, thorough and objective manner," and providing a report to the complainant at the end of the investigation process;
- a prohibition on retaliation against the complainant or witnesses;
- appropriate corrective actions, including but not limited to termination, to prevent and correct unlawful harassment or retaliation;
- "communication regarding the existence, resolution, and any consideration paid for the settlement of claims to the highest levels of the entity, such as reporting to the Board of Directors or Executive Committee"; and
- Regular "and effective" training programs for all employees and other individuals protected by and/or subject to the policies and procedures.

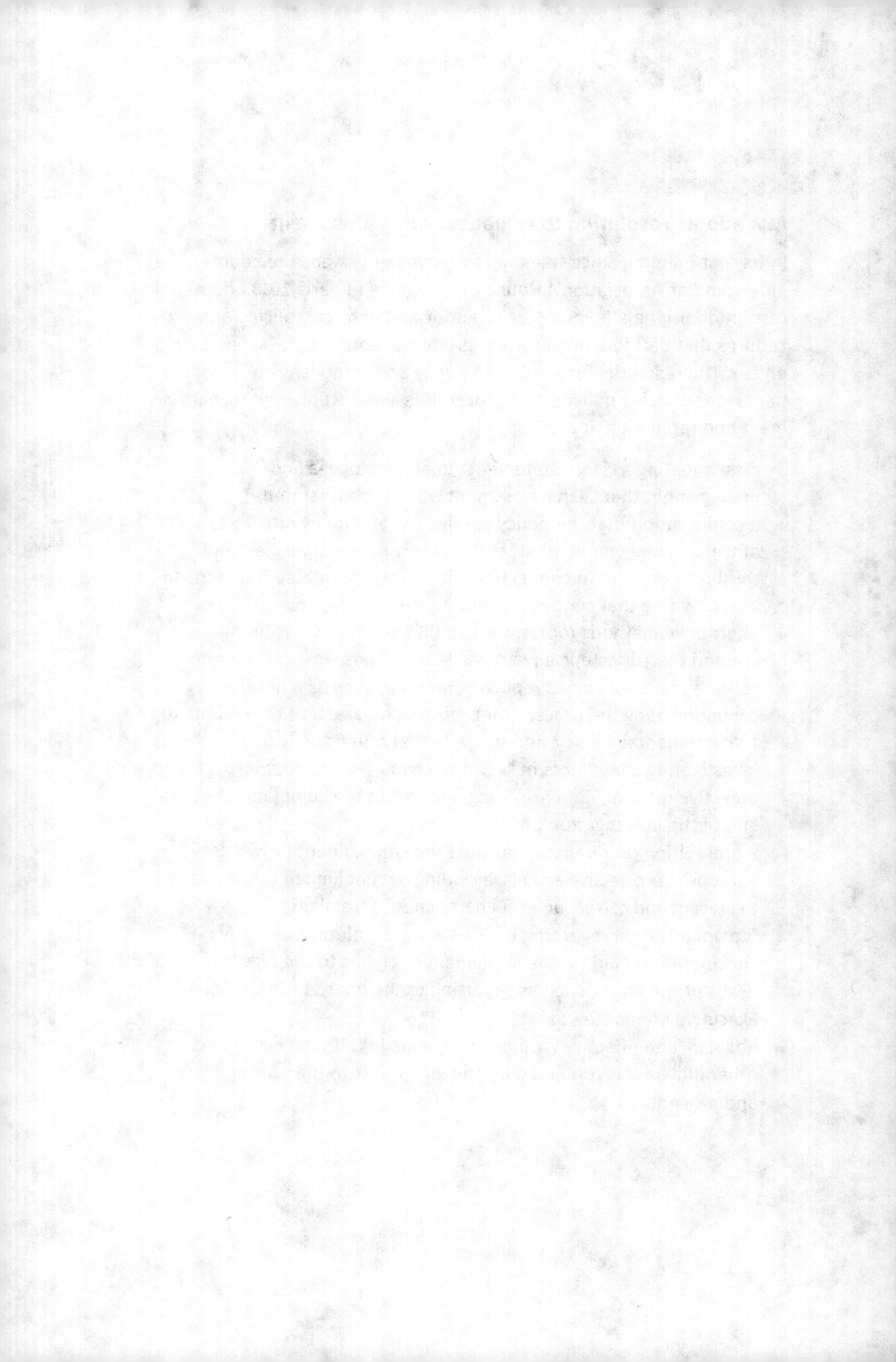

Chapter 5

Sexual harassment training

As part of your organization's bias-free workplace efforts, you developed and distributed a clear policy against workplace sexual harassment that provides several avenues for victims to complain. The policy encourages potential victims to come forward and makes clear that retaliation will not be tolerated. You also set up an internal procedure for investigating sexual harassment and adopted disciplinary measures to follow in the event the policy is violated. You distributed the policy to the entire workforce and posted it on bulletin boards and the company's intranet. Finally, you updated your organization's sexual harassment training tutorial and made sure everyone, from upper-level management to supervisory personnel to staff, signed off on the annual Power Point training.

Despite all this, sexual harassment in your workplace continues to be a problem. As a matter of fact, since the explosion of the #MeToo movement, you've seen an increase in sexual harassment complaints. You decide it's time to update your training, but how? Is face-to-face training more effective? Should you shut down the entire organization for half a day like Starbucks did to train everyone at one time? And what about this bystander intervention or workplace civility training you keep hearing about? Will any of it really make a difference?

Why hasn't sexual harassment training worked?

Having a comprehensive anti-harassment policy as well as complaint and disciplinary procedures in place to prevent workplace sexual harassment is critical, but it is just the beginning. Training is also an important tool in combatting sexual harassment. But many employers have been providing anti-harassment training for years. As a matter of fact, almost 75 percent of the HR professionals who responded to a 2018 XpertHR Workplace Sexual Harassment survey said their organizations currently offer sexual harassment prevention training.

And yet, as the #MeToo movement revealed, sexual harassment is still entrenched in too many workplaces, prompting some companies to rethink how they train their employees. For instance, after sexual harassment allegations led NBC News to fire its popular morning TV show anchor, it announced that it would not only require its employees to attend anti-harassment training in person, it would also conduct a culture assessment.

And in the wake of sexual harassment allegations by a former Uber engineer, a law firm hired by the ride-sharing company recommended, among other things, mandatory leadership training for senior leaders to combat implicit bias and encourage a culture in which everyone is heard and feels safe. The firm also recommended mandatory HR training on the effective handling of complaints, as well as mandatory manager training that would include a comprehensive, live training program focusing on diversity, inclusion, and unconscious bias.

> **Don't miss this!** *According to a December 2017 CNBC All-America Survey, 19 percent of American adults said they have been victims of sexual harassment in the workplace. Among men, the figure was 10 percent, while among women it jumped to 27 percent.*

Training overview

So what's going on, then? Has training really failed as a sexual harassment prevention tool? One problem, according to the EEOC's 2016 report from its Select Task Force on the Study of Harassment in the Workplace, is that much of the training conducted by employers over the last 30 years has been focused on avoiding liability in sexual harassment lawsuits rather than on preventing sexual harassment from occurring.

Legal reasons to train. For instance, there are several specific reasons from a legal perspective as to why employers have implemented sexual harassment training.

- **Prevent liability for supervisor harassment.** Training can assist an employer's ability to prove both that it acted *reasonably*, by teaching supervisors and employees workplace harassment prevention, and by showing that the employee acted *unreasonably* because he or she was educated on harassment and the organization's complaint procedure, yet failed to take appropriate action.
- **Prevent liability for coworker and nonemployee harassment.** Employees must learn that they have a duty to report sexual harassment themselves, so that the employer is given the opportunity to promptly correct the situation and, therefore, avoid liability. Additionally, supervisors must be taught to recognize and address workplace sexual harassment so that "known" harassment does not go uncorrected.
- **Prevent liability for punitive damages.** Documented training efforts can demonstrate an employer's strong commitment to a nondiscriminatory work environment—and as a result, prevent it from having to pay punitive damages.

While training methods vary from workplace to workplace—from small face-to-face training groups to larger seminars to online programs—employers often use training to educate employees on how to recognize sexual harassment and how to report it. There is little evidence, however, to show this actually works to prevent workplace sexual harassment.

> **Don't miss this!** *EEOC reporting statistics reveal that between 2011 and 2017, employers paid more than $250 million during its pre-litigation enforcement process as a result of employees alleging sex-based harassment.*

Reinforced behavior. What's more, according to Justine Tinkler, a University of Georgia researcher and sociologist, workplace sexual harassment policies and training can unintentionally reinforce traditional gender stereotypes and negative attitudes about women. Explains Tinkler, "The whole idea of trying to force a change in the way men and women interact with each other challenges the way that we think about what it means to be a man and what it means to be a woman, so we can get resistance to that message in complicated ways." In addition, results from a 2001 study entitled "The Unexpected Effects of a Sexual Harassment Educational Program" indicate that men who participated in a sexual harassment training program were less likely than other groups to perceive coercive sexual harassment, less willing to report it, and more likely to blame the victim.

Traditional compliance training

Does this mean that employers should scrap traditional sexual harassment training? Maybe not entirely. Effective training—training that educates the workforce on the law and company policies—is important. But training, notes the EEOC, is often done in a vacuum. To be effective, it must be part of a holistic harassment prevention effort by top leadership to establish a culture of respect in which harassment is not tolerated. In addition, it should be designed to fit the organization's specific workplace and workforce.

Training components. One of the primary goals of traditional sexual harassment compliance training is to effectively communicate the organization's clear policy against sexual harassment and other types of inappropriate workplace behavior. The training program should teach all employees about the organization's workplace harassment policy, including the complaint procedures to be followed and the multiple avenues in which harassment can be reported.

The workforce should also be trained on the process for investigating complaints and the disciplinary measures that may be taken against someone who engages in sexual harassment and/or inappropriate behavior. Train employees on what is and is not harassing behavior, as well as inappropriate behavior that, if unaddressed, may become unlawful harassment. Include specific descriptions and examples of harassing behavior.

> **Don't miss this!** According to attorney Chris Bourgeacq, of the Chris Bourgeacq Law Firm, it's better for an employer to be as specific as possible—using examples—when training employees on conduct to be avoided. This is no different that providing examples in safety training, Foreign Corrupt Practices Act training, or other training to avoid breaking the law. As to whether training should explain what is not legally defined as harassment but just poor behavior, he suggests that could have the unintended effect of misleading employees into thinking they're fine as long as the misbehavior doesn't rise to the level of harassment as it is legally defined.

It is important to make clear that it is each person's responsibility to report suspected harassment—whether they are a target of it or a witness to it—by following the organization's complaint procedure. Employees need to understand that the organization must be made aware of inappropriate conduct in order to promptly investigate and take whatever action is necessary to retain a harassment-free environment.

You cannot overstate the organization's commitment. Employees also need to know that any complaints will be handled as confidentially as possible and that anyone who complains of or reports harassment will not be subjected to retaliation.

✔ CHECKLIST: Effective harassment training

In its 2018 Proposed Enforcement Guidance on Unlawful Harassment, the EEOC recommends regular, interactive, comprehensive training of all employees to ensure that the workforce understands organizational rules, policies, procedures, and expectations, as well as the consequences of misconduct. Harassment training should be:

- ☐ Championed by senior leaders;
- ☐ Repeated and reinforced regularly;
- ☐ Provided to employees at every level and location of the organization;
- ☐ Provided in all languages commonly used by employees;
- ☐ Tailored to the specific workplace and workforce;
- ☐ Conducted by qualified, live, interactive trainers, or, if live training is not feasible, designed to include active engagement by participants; and
- ☐ Routinely evaluated by participants and revised as necessary.

Supervisory personnel. Because supervisors are required to proactively respond to and report harassment, they need to learn the seriousness of supervisor harassment; their duty to monitor the workplace and report harassment; and how to respond to a complaint of workplace harassment. The EEOC, in its 2018 proposed enforcement guidance, recommends that training for supervisors and managers additionally include:

- Information about how to prevent, identify, stop, report, and correct harassment. This includes identification of potential risk factors for harassment; easy-to-understand, realistic methods for addressing harassment; clear instructions about how to report harassment up the chain of command; and explanations regarding confidentiality rules for harassment complaints.
- An unequivocal statement that retaliation is prohibited and will not be tolerated.
- Explanations of the consequences of failing to fulfill their managerial responsibilities related to harassment, retaliation, and other prohibited conduct.

More than a compliance issue. But should employers do more? In response to a late 2017, early 2018 survey by the Next Concept Human Resource Association (NCHRA) and Waggl, only 32 percent of participants agreed that increased media attention around high-profile sexual harassment cases would make things easier for HR in the coming year. On the other hand, 90 percent agreed that the best way to eliminate workplace sexual harassment is to ensure higher standards for leaders. The survey responses, observed NCHRA's CEO, suggest that "Eliminating sexual harassment will require a cultural shift supported by relevant training around respect, communication, and work styles."

In addition to the more traditional approach, then, employers may want to consider additional alternative approaches to sexual harassment training. For instance, two alternative training methods—workplace civility training and bystander intervention training—are designed to address the culture of an organization in order to eliminate workplace sexual harassment.

Bystander intervention training

Relatively new to corporate America, bystander intervention training may not be familiar to a lot of employers. It's been successfully used outside the workplace, however, by colleges and the military, for instance, to combat sexual assault and domestic violence. The idea behind this type of training is that bystanders, who are witnesses to, rather than the target of, workplace sexual harassment, or who later learn about the harassment, can learn to be more than just passive bystanders.

Don't miss this! Research from the Australian Human Rights Commission suggests that one of the reasons bystander intervention training has been underutilized in the workplace is because harassers tend to actively hide their behavior, especially the more egregious forms of harassment. However, the Commission notes, evidence of the success of bystander intervention training in other areas suggests it may be highly effective in raising awareness of sexual harassment in the workplace and may also be effective in changing cultures of tolerance toward the harassment.

The training teaches employees not only how to recognize inappropriate conduct, but how to intervene, or interrupt it, when it does occur by providing them with different options on how to respond. As the Department of Justice's Office on Violence Against Women observes, a sense of responsibility gives the bystander motivation to step in and take action. An interruption or intervention can be something simple, such as dropping a book to create a distraction, and does not have to involve directly confronting the harasser.

> **Example:** Liam had noticed in the past that every time Gabe stopped by Brynn's desk, he rubbed her shoulders and told her she looked really hot. Although Brynn always looked embarrassed and uncomfortable, Liam never knew what to do. What if Brynn didn't mind Gabe's attention after all? Was it really something he should get involved in? And what was he supposed to do anyway? Then Liam attended bystander intervention training as part of his company's overall sexual harassment training. As a result, he realized that even though he was uncomfortable with the situation, he wasn't powerless. The training provided him with several options on how to deal with this type of behavior. The next time Gabe stopped by Brynn's desk, Liam stood up and asked Brynn if she wanted to grab a cup of coffee with him. When Brynn accepted his invitation, Gabe simply walked away.

In implementing bystander intervention training, employers should also stress that their policy against retaliation applies to any employee who does intervene to stop what the employee perceives to be inappropriate workplace conduct.

> **Don't miss this!** According to the EEOC, organizational culture starts from the top. But reinforcing that culture can and must come from the bottom, middle, and everywhere else in between. Bystander intervention training provides that reinforcement in a particularly concrete manner.

Most bystander intervention trainings, notes the EEOC Select Task Force on the Study of Harassment in the Workplace, employ at least four strategies:

- *Create awareness:* Enable bystanders to recognize potentially problematic behaviors.
- *Create a sense of collective responsibility:* Motivate bystanders to step in and take action when they observe problematic behaviors.
- *Create a sense of empowerment:* Conduct skills-building exercises to provide bystanders with the skills and confidence to intervene as appropriate.
- *Provide resources:* Provide bystanders with resources they can call upon and that support their intervention.

Example: What are some of the ways witnesses to workplace sexual harassment might help? A December 2017 article, Here's how to help if you witness sexual harassment at work, from Moneyish.com, suggests the following approaches—although it cautions that not all approaches work for all situations, and that actual bystander intervention training is recommended:

- *Confront the harasser. Because many workplace harassers don't appear to recognize their behavior is inappropriate, bystanders in some instances may confront the harasser directly. If so, it is important to "be specific about the conduct, be specific about the fact that it's making people uncomfortable, and be specific that it needs to stop." This approach does not require the bystander to identify the person who is being harassed, for example—the bystander may just say that the observed behavior is "making people uncomfortable." And the confrontation does not need to be angry or threatening; it can instead be couched as "hey, maybe you don't know that you're making people feel uneasy."*

- *Run interference. Often, sexual harassment occurs when a harasser gets his or her target alone. If the bystander either has an impression that a situation looks unwelcome or has heard rumors of harassing behavior, the bystander may run interference for the target. "Insert yourself into the conversation;" "take the seat next to the person;" don't let the harasser "have that one-on-one engagement."*

- *Throw the target a lifeline. Similar to the running interference approach is to simply interrupt the interaction with an invitation to do something else. This has the advantage of giving the potential target the option—and some perceived power—to take back control of the situation.*

  These approaches are not solutions, though. They are only a temporary fix.

- *Go to a manager. "If you're a non-management worker uncomfortable approaching the harasser—due to their personality or stature within the company, perhaps—then the best thing to do is go to somebody in some position of authority," the article suggests.*

- **Talk to the target.** *A bystander may not feel comfortable approaching the target, and the target may not feel comfortable being approached, the article points out. However, if you approach the target, "speak with empathy, realize their reaction may not be what you expected, understand they may be unwilling to talk," and don't expect that you can "solve their pain." But you might help the target understand that he or she is not alone and that approaching someone else might be a way forward.*

- **Take contemporaneous notes.** *Finally, the "most effective thing" is to "record details in real time of harassment you've witnessed, then make yourself available to testify should your colleague file a complaint." "Send a text to yourself — that's a good way of making sure you remember the details that may become important."*

Workplace civility training

Employers may also want to consider workplace civility training, which focuses on creating a culture of civility, in addition to traditional workplace sexual harassment training. Workplace civility training is more established than bystander intervention training. As a matter of fact, many employers use it to combat bullying or other workplace conflicts, as this type of training focuses on promoting respect and civility in the workplace generally.

Don't miss this! *According to researchers, incivility is often an antecedent to workplace harassment, as it creates a climate of "general derision and disrespect" in which harassing behaviors are tolerated, the EEOC observes. For example, in studies of attorneys and court employees, researchers found significant correlations between incivility and gender harassment. Researchers also have found that uncivil behaviors can often "spiral" into harassing behaviors.*

Instead of focusing on what employees should not do, this type of training promotes positive behaviors like civility, respect, and trust. While it may include a discussion of appropriate and inappropriate workplace behavior, it might also include training on interpersonal skills, conflict resolution, and effective supervisory techniques.

Notes Anne Barry, the Director of Operations at Aureon HR in a December 2017 blog, "almost every organization offers harassment training, but that may not always be enough. Harassment training usually shows the extreme behaviors, but even negative behavior that isn't considered 'harassment' can be detrimental to a culture." Barry believes it is beneficial to go beyond the normal training and offer a course in civility training. "This seeks to present the concept in a different way and show how important and valuable being civil and treating others with respect is in the workplace. This also helps foster a culture where it's expected and natural to be nice to each other, and it even starts with who you hire."

Don't miss this! *Although the EEOC believes that workplace civility training could provide an important complement to compliance training, it warns that some broad workplace "civility codes," which may be read to limit or restrict certain forms of employee speech about the workplace, may raise issues under the National Labor Relations Act.*

In 2017, the EEOC launched two trainings for employers that, rather than focusing on traditional compliance training, focus on respect, acceptable workplace conduct, and the types of behaviors that contribute to an inclusive workplace. According to EEOC Commissioner Chai Feldblum, "A strong training program is a critical piece of a holistic harassment prevention effort. We know that workplace incivility often acts as a 'gateway drug' to workplace harassment. These trainings, therefore, provide employees with the specific skills they need to act respectfully and to intervene when they observe disrespectful or abusive behavior. In short, the program is designed to stop improper behavior before it ever rises to the level of illegal harassment."

According to a fact sheet provided by the EEOC, the training modules – *Leading for Respect* (for supervisors) and *Respect in the Workplace* (for all employees) – go beyond traditional harassment prevention training. The modules contain sections on the concept of respect, the spectrum of workplace behaviors (including respectful, uncivil, abusive, and illegal behaviors), employer policies and procedures, fairness, bystander intervention, effective coaching, and how to provide and receive feedback. Most trainings on harassment prevention focus on what employees should not do, but these focus on what employees should do, the EEOC stresses.

The modules focus on the values of respect and fairness. Each program facilitates discussion among participants about the behaviors and words that generate respect and their responsibility for contributing to respect in the workplace. Participants learn how to provide and receive feedback about behavior that is uncivil and disrespectful, and supervisors learn specific skills for handling difficult issues.

When to train

Although a handful of states have laws requiring certain employers provide sexual harassment training, these laws vary in terms of how often training is required, how long the training should be, and who must be trained. Most states, however, do not currently require that private employers provide sexual harassment training for their workforce. As a result of the #MeToo movement, however, many states and municipalities are considering legislation that would include mandatory sexual harassment training.

How often, then, should employers provide sexual harassment training? To ensure that an employer's communication efforts are reasonable, training should occur regularly. What does that mean? It is best to train both employees and supervisors upon hire as part of their orientation. Then train at least annually, if not more frequently.

If a sexual harassment complaint has been made or if harassment has been observed, it may be necessary to retrain the entire workforce or those employees who may be lacking in the necessary understanding of appropriate behavior. If a complaint is found to have merit, this is a clear warning signal to HR that training efforts should be re-evaluated for effectiveness.

Don't miss this! As noted by the EEOC's Select Task Force on the Study of Harassment in the Workplace, employees understand that an organization's devotion of time and resources to any effort reflects the organization's commitment to that effort. Training is no different. If anti-harassment trainings are held once a year (or once every other year), employees will not believe that preventing harassment is a high priority for the employer.

Conversely, if anti-harassment trainings are regularly scheduled events in which key information is reinforced, that will send the message that the goal of the training is important. While this is one area where, in general, repetition is a good thing, the Task Force cautions against simply repeating the same training over and over, which risks becoming a rote exercise. Rather, employers should consider training that is varied and dynamic in style, form, and content.

Who to train

It used to be sufficient to train managers and supervisors about workplace sexual harassment. However, that is no longer the case. Employers should train *all* employees on sexual harassment prevention.

Carmen Feinberg, an HR executive level consultant and Forbes Human Resources Council Contributor, suggests conducting sexual harassment training for employees and supervisors separately. "Use a variety of methods to communicate the policy to management and employees. Conduct formal training as least twice annually for managers and supervisors," she advises. "Separating groups is smart because you want to inform all staff what to do if they feel sexually harassed or witness sexual harassment, yet you also want to inform your managers what they must do when they receive a complaint of sexual harassment."

Accommodations in training. HR has an obligation under the Americans with Disabilities Act to provide employees with disabilities the opportunity to participate in training. Training opportunities cannot be denied because of the need to make reasonable accommodations to the training process, unless accommodations would be an undue hardship.

✔ CHECKLIST: Accommodation suggestions

Accommodations that may be necessary, depending on the needs of particular workers, include:

- ☐ accessible locations and facilities for people with mobility disabilities;
- ☐ interpreters and note-takers for workers who have hearing impairments;
- ☐ materials in accessible formats;
- ☐ readers for people who have visual impairments, learning disabilities, and cognitive disabilities;
- ☐ captions for people who are hearing-impaired, and voice-overs for people who are visually impaired when audiovisual materials are used;
- ☐ good general illumination for people with visual impairments; and
- ☐ clarification of concepts presented for people who have reading or other disabilities.

Evaluation

It is important to routinely evaluate training programs to ensure they are accomplishing their intended goals. The evaluation should assess whether or not the training enhanced employees' knowledge and understanding of workplace sexual harassment, reaffirmed the organization's policy, led to employee behavior change, and ultimately reinforced the culture of workplace civility.

Follow-up approaches could include surveys or small group discussions or interviews with participants. Long-term follow-up might be measured by reviewing performance appraisals and grievance and complaint rates.

> **Don't miss this!** Employers should obviously not keep doing something that does not work, the EEOC Task Force stresses. Trainers should not only do the training, but should evaluate the results of the training, as well. This should involve more than handing a questionnaire to participants immediately after the training asking if they found the training to be helpful.
>
> "Evaluations are most effective if they are done some time after the training and participants are asked questions such as whether the training changed their own behaviors or behaviors they have observed in the workplace. The evaluation should occur on a regular basis so that the training can be modified, if need be. Similarly, training evaluation should incorporate feedback from all levels of an organization, most notably, the rank-and-file employees who are being trained, lest 'evaluation' becomes a senior leadership 'echo chamber.'"

Changing the culture

As the EEOC points out in its 2018 proposed guidance, when evaluating or implementing a training program, it is important to keep in mind that while leadership, accountability, and strong harassment policies and complaint systems are essential components of a successful harassment prevention strategy, employees must be aware of them. The best way to ensure awareness is through regular, interactive, comprehensive training. Employees at all levels of the organization must understand the organizational rules, policies, procedures, and expectations, as well as the consequences of misconduct.

But that's just the beginning. As a 2018 nationwide study by the National Academies of Sciences, Engineering, and Medicine reveals, "Attending to an organization's climate is crucial to preventing and addressing harassment because organizational climate is the greatest predictor of sexual harassment."

Echoing this sentiment, the EEOC's Task Force also observed that "Workplace culture has the greatest impact on allowing harassment to flourish, or conversely, in preventing harassment." Accordingly, the Task Force explains, effective training must be part of a holistic culture of non-harassment that starts at the top. The Task Force recommends that employers offer not only compliance training on a regular basis, they must dedicate sufficient resources to train middle management and first line supervisors to respond to workplace sexual harassment *before the harassment reaches a legally actionable level*. In addition, the Task Force recommends that employers also consider including workplace civility training and bystander intervention training as part of their holistic prevention program.

> **Don't miss this!** *"Culture always trumps compliance," notes Johnny C. Taylor, president and CEO of the Society of Human Resource Management, in a statement submitted to the California Legislature's Joint Committee on Rules Subcommittee on Sexual Harassment Prevention and Response. Explaining that rules, education, and training are necessary but will never be enough, Taylor emphasized that "an organization's culture is more than being a nice place to work, where everyone is engaged and happy. We must take the concept far beyond that, to where culture—not HR policies—represents who we are and what we believe as an organization."*

Chapter 6

Investigating harassment

Dimitri enters the HR office early one morning and asks if he can speak to someone in private. You usher him into your office and ask him to take a seat. Dimitri seems very nervous. Before you have a chance to ask him why he's there, he blurts out that he is having problems with a coworker and doesn't know what to do. He says, "I may not be as manly as the rest of the crew, but I am not like that." Dimitri shows you a cartoon that shows two men in a sexually explicit pose. Someone has handwritten the word "Dimitri" on the cartoon, along with an arrow pointing to one of the men. You ask Dimitri where he found the cartoon and he says, "You know what? Never mind. This was a mistake, I think I should go." And then he leaves. What should you do? What if Dimitri is unwilling to provide further details? Even if he does, what steps should you take based on his story?

Becoming aware of harassment

Employers may become aware of potential workplace sexual harassment in many ways. Some of the more common sources include:

- A workplace rumor.
- An anonymous complaint.
- A complaint by another employee or someone outside of the organization.
- A complaint by the victim to a member of management—typically the employee's manager or supervisor—or to another person in a position to do something about it, such as a security guard.
- A complaint by the victim to HR.
- An allegation made in social media.
- Observance of the harassment by management, a coworker, or by a member of HR.

Social media complaints. Sexual harassment complaints can also arise through employee or workplace social media. The prevalence of social media complicates an already difficult investigation process, notes Sherman and Howard attorney Brooke Colaizzi. "If an employer becomes aware of a complaint, even if only through social media, it must very carefully consider what steps it needs to take." Those steps, she suggested, may include:

- Approaching the complainant, if the identity of the complainant is known.
- All-employee meetings or communications encouraging employees to come forward with concerns.
- Monitoring to ensure that preventative practices, including policy dissemination and training, are actually working to prevent harassment.

Colaizzi, however, cautioned employers against assuming that because the complaint arose on social media or did not come through the "proper" channels, there is no obligation to respond. Employers should treat a social media complaint the same as any other complaint.

> **Don't miss this!** Another way that an organization may become aware of workplace sexual harassment is by the receipt of a formal complaint from the EEOC or other administrative agency. Because of the various legal implications created by the government's involvement, special investigatory precautions may be necessary. Therefore, it is best for HR to immediately consult legal counsel for guidance once a formal charge of harassment has been received.

Regardless of how an employer finds out about a sexual harassment allegation, it must respond immediately. Starting the investigation one day after a complaint is filed would be considered prompt action by the employer, but waiting two months would not.

One of the biggest mistakes employers can make is to ignore or improperly respond to sexual harassment in the workplace. It is unlikely that the organization is intentionally ignoring harassment. Rather, a worker may be embarrassed or scared about inappropriate behavior and therefore not come right out and clearly say what has occurred. Meanwhile HR professionals, concerned about employee privacy rights, are cautious about making additional inquiries. Therefore, it is crucial that employers create an atmosphere where employees feel comfortable raising issues concerning sexually harassing behavior.

Example: *Elliott keeps brushing up against his coworker, Yelena, telling her she looks really hot, making suggestive comments to her, and more recently touching her inappropriately. When she first met Elliot, Yelena thought he was cute and she went out with him one time. But now, she just wants him to stop. She feels uncomfortable talking to HR, however, about the nature of his actions. Not only is she embarrassed, she's worried they will think she "led him on" and blame her. But things are getting worse. So instead she complains that Elliot makes her feel "uncomfortable" and she doesn't want to be around him.*

If HR dismisses Yelena's complaint as insignificant, she probably will not feel comfortable raising the issue again. But if Elliot's behavior continues and is severe or pervasive enough to be considered unlawful sexual harassment, the employer could be in legal trouble because Yelena complained about the behavior and the employer failed to investigate and take prompt, corrective action.

The initial complaint

Often, an employer becomes aware of potential sexual harassment because an employee brings a complaint to HR or to another member of management. Because this might be the first time the conduct is made known, it is vital that the person who receives a complaint of sexual harassment—whether an HR professional, a manager, or a supervisor—be prepared to respond properly by taking the following steps: Listen, encourage, ask questions, document, explain, and respond.

Listen. To effectively address a sexual harassment complaint, the person taking the complaint must be a good listener, able to create an atmosphere where employees feel comfortable raising sensitive issues. Every complaint of harassment must be taken seriously, no matter how silly or insignificant the behavior may seem at first to be. Don't assume someone is being too sensitive or overreacting. Try to see things through the employee's perspective.

Don't miss this! Sexual harassment is not an easy topic for any employee to bring up. The employee may be embarrassed, afraid of losing his or her job, or just an ineffective communicator. Listen for code words when someone complains about another's behavior. For instance, does he or she "feel uncomfortable" or "uneasy?" Is he or she asking to not have to work with a particular person because they "don't get along?" Does a coworker "treat her funny" or "act creepy around him?"

Encourage. Try to make the employee feel comfortable while maintaining a professional attitude. Acknowledge that bringing a sexual harassment complaint is a difficult thing to do and that it is normal for the employee to feel uneasy. Reassure him or her that the information will be kept as confidential as possible, but do not promise it will remain a "secret."

Ask questions. Ask who did what to whom, when, where, how, and why. But refrain from offering an opinion. Find out as well what the employee would like to see happen as a result of the complaint.

Document. Immediately create a written record of the employee's statements. Do not wait to document. It is important that records of a sexual harassment complaint reflect exactly what was said. Ask the person complaining to review and sign your documentation to reflect that it is accurate. If the employee is unwilling to provide a written statement, simply take note of that fact and continue with the interview anyway.

Explain. Explain the workplace sexual harassment policy to the employee. Provide assurances that no retaliation or negative employment action will be taken against the employee for making the complaint. Answer any questions that he or she may have.

Respond. Immediately report the conversation as outlined in your organization's sexual harassment policy. If you are charged with the authority to initiate an investigation into the matter, take the necessary steps to do so.

The reluctant employee

What if an employee complains about sexual harassment but asks that his or her complaint be kept secret? Even if a person who reports workplace harassment asks that no action be taken, an employer that does nothing in response can be held liable for the harassment. HR is now aware of the situation and must investigate and take any necessary corrective action. HR should therefore explain to the employee that the employer has a strict policy forbidding sexual harassment in the workplace and has a legal duty to investigate the problem now that it has been raised. Assure the employee that the matter will be handled as discreetly as possible and that no negative employment action will result from the employee's complaint. Then investigate the complaint.

> **Don't miss this!** *An investigation is obviously hindered if the employee refuses to give any further information about the conduct. This makes it especially important for HR to document the employee's failure to cooperate, document any answers to questions the employee may have provided, and document any further investigatory actions that are taken by the organization. HR should also encourage the employee to come forward again if the harassment continues and continue to follow up with the employee.*

Think back to Dimitri. He came to you complaining of harassment but became reluctant during your conversation. This is obviously a sensitive issue for Dimitri and, as such, it was probably very difficult for him to come to you in the first place. It is important to reassure Dimitri that the organization will handle the situation as discreetly as possible and protect him from retaliation. At the same time, Dimitri must understand that HR will be investigating the matter so that necessary steps can be taken to end any inappropriate behavior in the workplace.

The delayed complaint

What if an employee reports harassment that supposedly occurred several years ago? Take the complaint seriously and investigate as you would a current claim. In addition to the basic information you would ask of the employee, in the case of a delayed complaint, also ask if any similar activity has occurred recently. Ask whether some form of retaliation occurred because of the incident. Especially in the #MeToo era, individuals may be willing to bring forward issues now that they were too fearful to address even a few years ago. Accordingly, it is important to investigate to see if other workers have or had similar complaints. Experts on harassment warn that in many cases there will be a pattern of harassing behavior by a supervisor or coworker that is repeated over the years with different employees.

Worst case scenario

Sheri's supervisor made unwanted sexual advances towards her, his secretary, for a number of years. She never reported his conduct. He was warned twice for harassing other employees and eventually fired after his conduct toward the secretary came to light. Sheri later brought a sexual harassment claim against the employer and the supervisor individually. While the lower court dismissed the case, finding that the employer had shown that it should not be legally liable for the harassment because it exercised reasonable care to eliminate it and the secretary failed to take advantage of its policies and procedures—she never reported it, remember—a federal appellate court sent the case back for a jury to decide whether the employer acted with reasonable care to detect and eliminate the harassment and whether the secretary acted reasonably in not reporting the harassment should be decided by a jury.

Reasonable safeguards? The employer maintained a written anti-harassment policy, but there was evidence that it had turned a blind eye to harassment by the supervisor: He had made inappropriate physical advances to a number of employees, including two women who were in a position to discipline him for his behavior. Although one of them raised the issue with executives, no reprimand was issued.

Failure to report. Moreover, Sheri did not necessarily act unreasonably by failing to report the supervisor's behavior. Mere failure to report is not always unreasonable. Here, Sheri testified that she needed the job and was afraid of retaliation. She and her supervisor worked together alone one day a week, and he monitored her on the other days. The power imbalance between the two could have contributed to Sheri's fear of speaking up. Also, her supervisor became ill-tempered when she tried to assert herself (for example, by not answering his phone calls on days she was not working). In other words, the employee's fear was not just a general fear of retaliation, but was specific and supported by evidence.

In addition, Sheri's supervisor had discouraged her from using the anti-harassment policy by repeatedly telling her that she could not trust the managers to whom she would have reported the conduct. She believed reporting his behavior would be futile since the employer knew of his past harassment, yet the conduct continued. Under the circumstances, a jury could find that her non-reporting was reasonable, and the employer would have to defend itself in front of a jury.

It is possible that the employee cannot go to a government agency or sue in court because too much time has passed under EEOC or other legal rules for filing charges or filing a lawsuit. However, HR can never be too sure that there is no legal risk; it is also possible that other employees may have claims that they have not yet brought forward, but which may be timely. More importantly, remember that there is no "time limit" on your organization's policy against sexual harassment. Regardless of your legal liability, sexual or any other type of harassment can and does poison a working environment, resulting in increased turnover and lost productivity at the very least. So the passage of time is no reason to dismiss the importance of a complaint.

The top performer

What if the complaint is made against an executive or top performer in the organization? Executives and top performers can pose unique challenges for employers, especially when the accused harasser has a significant impact on the organization's bottom line. HR, however, must treat a complaint against an executive or a top performer in the same manner it would treat a complaint against any other employee. All employees are equally required to comply with the same laws and policies, and an employer's investigation and follow-up should be equally vigorous when handling complaints about senior leaders and top performers.

The EEOC addressed the problem of the top performer—who the Commission's Select Task Force on the Study of Harassment in the Workplace 2016 report calls "superstars"—by pointing out that some of these individuals "are privileged with higher income, better accommodations, and different expectations. That privilege can lead to a self-view that they are above the rules, which can foster mistreatment. Psychologists have detailed how power can make an individual feel uninhibited and thus more likely to engage in inappropriate behaviors. In short, superstar status can be a breeding ground for harassment."

Moreover, employers may find themselves weighing the productivity of a "superstar" harasser *solely* against the costs of his or her being reported. But the EEOC cited a Harvard Business School study that found "the profit consequences of so-called 'toxic workers'—*specifically including* those who are 'top performers'—is a net negative." Avoiding these toxic workers might save a company more than twice as much as the increased output generated by a top performer, the study suggested.

Don't miss this! "When a top performer is accused, that employee is not excused from abiding by the same laws and any company policies addressing sexual harassment," notes attorney Chris Bourgeacq, the Chris Bourgeacq Law Firm. *"But when either the company's livelihood, or a substantial revenue source, or the company's brand is at stake, it is even more important to conduct a thorough investigation and leave no stone unturned to determine the truth of the allegations and any defenses."*

Starting the investigation

Once inappropriate conduct is reported or an employer otherwise becomes aware of a problem, it is necessary to conduct an immediate internal investigation. The best policy is to investigate all complaints and appearances of workplace sexual harassment and to make a determination based purely on the facts. The quicker the response to a workplace sexual harassment complaint, the lower the risk of liability. Also, unnecessarily delaying or even extending the investigation traumatizes an organization and makes witness testimony increasingly unreliable.

Example: Kristen, a counter worker at a fast food restaurant, complained to Howard, the store manager that Skip, a kitchen employee, was sexually harassing her. A couple of weeks later, Howard asked Tyler, a shift manager at the restaurant, to look into things. Tyler was not familiar with the restaurant's sexual harassment policy and had never even been involved in an investigation before. On top of that, he was leaving on vacation the next day. When he returned eight days later, he met with both Skip and Kristen individually. Because he knew both of them, he only talked to them for 10-15 minutes each and never took notes. Nor did he contact any other coworkers. He did submit a written memo to Howard, though, explaining that Skip denied everything, claiming instead that Kristen was just mad because he wouldn't go out with her, and Tyler thought Skip seemed pretty believable. Under these circumstances, the employer did not conduct an adequate investigation.

What are the steps?

The goal of a workplace harassment investigation is to gather *all* of the facts so that the employer can determine whether inappropriate conduct did or did not occur. These are the general steps to follow, followed by details as to each step:

- Obtain relevant information.
- Conduct the interviews.
- Document the investigation.
- Maintain confidentiality to the extent possible.
- Protect the accused and the accuser.

Who should investigate?

In many cases, HR will be responsible for the investigation. HR professionals must be thoroughly trained before being assigned investigative duties, however. This should include learning the skills that are required for interviewing witnesses and evaluating credibility.

Do the individuals tasked with conducting internal investigations have a clear understanding of what constitutes workplace sexual harassment? In particular, if he or she has not already done so, the person who will be conducting the investigation must become familiar with the definition of workplace sexual harassment and examples of behaviors that have been found to be sexual harassment. And, of course, the investigator must be impartial, objective, fair, and circumspect.

Example: Brandy, an administrative assistant at a dialysis clinic, complained to James, the clinical coordinator, about the repeated sexual comments and conduct by her supervisor, Richard. Among other things, Richard called her his "work wife" and his "slave," rubbed her shoulders as she worked, and positioned himself so she backed into his crotch when she moved boxes. He also made sure to point out to his female staff that he could fire them at any time.

Fed up, Brandy quit. She also wrote a note to higher-level executives detailing the harassment and they responded by putting Janice, an HR manager, who was also Richard's "dear friend," in charge of the investigation. That investigation consisted entirely of an interview with Richard, who denied everything. Janice even failed to look into Brandy's claim that Richard had sexually harassed other women in the clinic. Under these circumstances, the investigation was far from a thorough, neutral process required in response to such serious accusations and undermined the employer's claim that it acted reasonably to promptly correct any sexually harassing behavior.

> **Don't miss this!** *What is the best process for handling sexual harassment complaints? The answer, observes Jackson Lewis attorney Stephanie Adler-Paindiris, is very fact specific. "In general," she recommends, "a company should have dedicated people who are trained regularly on conducting harassment investigations. It must also take immediate action and communicate with the complainant with respect to timing and the outcome." While in many cases it may be unwise for every manager or supervisor to be responsible for investigating complaints, "those individuals need to know where to go to report conduct they have seen or complaints they have received."*

Experts recommend that two investigators be assigned to investigate a sexual harassment investigation, especially for interviewing the complaining individual, the witnesses, and the accused individual—one to conduct the interviews, the other to take notes and provide support. In addition, a good practice is to make sure at least one of the two investigators is of the same gender as the complainant.

It is also important to assign investigators who do not have any relationship with the complaining employee, any witnesses, or the accused individual. In small organizations, this may present a problem, and you should consider whether or not it is prudent to have an outside firm conduct the investigation.

✔ CHECKLIST: What to consider during an investigation

- ☐ Your organization's sexual harassment policy, code of conduct, and any reporting processes it has in place;
- ☐ the frequency of the conduct that the employee has complained about;
- ☐ its severity;
- ☐ whether it is physically threatening or humiliating, or offensive comments only; and
- ☐ whether it unreasonably interferes with an employee's work performance.

In some organizations, HR may coordinate investigations with an in-house attorney. Also, HR may coordinate with the security department, especially if those departments contain staff with prior law enforcement background and training.

Another alternative is to ask an outside attorney to conduct the investigation. Although an expensive option, putting an attorney in charge of a workplace harassment investigation may show that the organization wants objectivity and is concerned about the seriousness of the charge. In the event the charge is against a senior member of management, utilizing outside attorneys may be the best strategy to avoid conflict of interest charges.

> **Don't miss this!** *When is it a good idea to handle an investigation internally, rather than hiring an outside investigator? The answer, says attorney Chris Bourgeacq, varies depending on the size and resources of the organization. "It's always more efficient, and sometimes more productive, to handle investigations internally. But sometimes, where there are high-risk situations, it's better to use a third-party investigator to provide more objectivity and back-up for leadership."*

Obtaining relevant information

The goal of the investigation is to gather all relevant information to help determine whether improper behavior has occurred. The employer must identify and obtain the information quickly.

What should it be looking for? Consider any information that will help verify facts as well as help identify persons who should be interviewed and what questions should be asked. Begin by reviewing the personnel files of the complainant, the alleged harasser, and any witnesses. Are there any notes regarding the incident? Any prior complaints? Make sure you have an initial list of appropriate individuals to interview; interviews may reveal new individuals to contact.

Seek out relevant information throughout the investigation by repeatedly asking witnesses and anyone else involved whether or not they have any additional information or documentation—or know of anyone else who does—that would be helpful in resolving the matter.

> ### ★ Best practices
>
> i-Sight, a software provider of case management solutions for incidents and investigations, recommends these reminders as a sexual harassment investigation begins:
>
> - Ensure the complainant knows that the company is taking his or her complaint seriously; be courteous and professional.
> - Conduct all investigation interviews in a private place, away from other employees *and* management.
> - Keep details of the case confidential; be discreet about the allegations as well as the identities of the complainant, the accused, and other witnesses, but do not promise confidentiality to anyone.
> - Explain the company's anti-retaliation policy to *every person you speak to* during the investigation and encourage them to report any retaliatory behavior they experience.
> - Take statements from interviewees when appropriate. Statements can be valuable evidence that supports or refutes the complainant's story.
> - Assess the credibility of *each interviewee and document* your assessment in your notes.

Conducting the interviews

The complainant

Often, the person to whom a complaint is brought initially (a manager or supervisor; an HR representative) is not the same person who will conduct the investigation. Clearly, not all information will necessarily be covered in that initial meeting. The following are some tips on interviewing the complaining employee once an investigation into workplace harassment has begun. These tips are applicable either during the initial meeting or in a follow-up meeting once an investigator has been assigned. If two investigators are participating, decide who will conduct the interview and who will take notes or record the discussion.

1. Get details. Ask the employee for specific details regarding the alleged workplace harassment. Acknowledge the sensitivity of the situation, however. You may need to reassure the complainant that the company is taking the allegations seriously and preventing additional harassing conduct. Include questions regarding:

- the type of conduct and its frequency;
- what specifically was said or done;
- where it occurred;
- the dates on which the conduct occurred; and
- the time period over which the conduct occurred.

Find out whether or not there was a pattern of previous episodes; was the person bringing the complaint aware of similar behavior by the accused towards any other employee?

> **Don't miss this!** It is helpful to prepare a detailed chronology. This will help you analyze whether there might have been certain events that triggered the complaint—for example, a denial of promotion, pay raise, or a transfer.

2. Understand the context. Get the specific context in which the conduct occurred, including the nature and general description of the work area and the specific location. Find out whether the conduct occurred at a work-related function, during working time, or after hours.

Also determine the time frame between the occurrence of the alleged conduct, its effect on the complainant, and the time when the complainant made the report. If there was a time lag between the occurrence and the report, find out why the complainant waited before reporting the situation. A plausible explanation may be the employee's fear, either of retaliation or simple embarrassment.

> **Don't miss this!** According to the EEOC, employers need to understand the larger context of how employees typically respond when they experience harassment in the workplace. Do they seek legal relief?
>
> In its Task Force report from 2016, the EEOC noted that "based on the empirical data, the extent of non-reporting is striking." Specifically, common workplace-based responses by those who experience sex-based harassment are to
>
> - avoid the harasser (33% to 75%);
> - deny or downplay the gravity of the situation (54% to 73%); or
> - attempt to ignore, forget or endure the behavior (44% to 70%).

In many cases, targets of harassment neither complain nor confront their harasser. Instead, "the least common response of either men or women to harassment is to take some formal action—either to report the harassment internally or file a formal legal complaint." According to several studies cited by the agency, approximately 70 percent of individuals who experienced harassment never spoke with a supervisor, manager, or union representative about the harassing conduct.

The EEOC report said studies have found that 6% to 13% of individuals who experience harassment file a formal complaint; "on average, anywhere from 87% to 94% of individuals did not file a formal complaint."

Employees who experience harassment fail to report it or file a complaint because they are concerned they will face these reactions from their employers:

- *disbelief of their claim;*
- *inaction on their claim;*
- *receipt of blame for causing the offending actions;*
- *social retaliation (humiliation, ostracism, disdain); and*
- *professional retaliation, such as damage to their career and reputation.*

These fears are well-founded, said the EEOC: "In many work environments, the most 'reasonable' course of action for the victim to take is to avoid reporting the harassment."

3. Understand the impact. Determine the effect of the conduct on the complainant.

- Identify what harm the conduct caused.
  - For example, were there financial or economic effects?
  - Did the complainant miss work or visit the doctor?
  - What about psychological effects like sleeplessness, loss of appetite, depression, or anxiety?
- Was the conduct received as a joke?
- Was it really unwelcome?
- Did it embarrass, frighten, or humiliate the complainant?

Don't miss this! Often, employees state that, while they may have acted as if they were not offended by harassment, they acted that way out of fear or because they felt threatened or intimidated. It is important to remember that the real issue is whether the behavior was unwelcome. Probe gently to get as much information as possible.

4. Find out what the complainant wants. Try to find out how the employee wants the situation resolved. It may be hard for him or her to come up with a succinct answer; in fact, it's possible that the complainant has never considered that question.

Probe further by finding out:

- Can the employee continue to work for or with the accused?
- Can the employee be productive?
- Will it be embarrassing or awkward for the employee, enough so that it will interfere with the employee's ability to do the job?
- Does the employee need counseling?

5. Explain the next steps. Explain that the charges are serious and that the employer (or an independent outside investigator) will conduct a thorough investigation before reaching any conclusions. Assure the employee that he or she will not be retaliated against for making the complaint. Keep the employee up to date on the status of the investigation, as appropriate, while it is still in progress.

Don't miss this! Make no statements about the accused's character, job performance, or family life, either to excuse or condemn the alleged behavior. The interviewer's job is to listen. If the accused were to sue for defamation, negative comments by an interviewer might be enough evidence for a finding of "malice" or spitefulness on the part of the employer. Malice wipes out the legal privilege that employers have to lawfully discuss these kinds of situations internally.

6. Get a written statement. Ask the employee to provide the details of the complaint in writing. If the employee is reluctant to write it down, don't argue, but continue your documentation. Make a note of the employee's reluctance to provide a written statement and specify the employee's concerns, including any facts to support those concerns.

Don't miss this! *The following are examples of EEOC-approved questions that may be appropriate to ask the complainant:*

- *Who, what, when, where, and how: Who committed the alleged harassment? What exactly occurred or was said? When did it occur and is it still ongoing? Where did it occur? How often did it occur? How did it affect you?*
- *How did you react? What response did you make when the incident(s) occurred or afterwards?*
- *How did the harassment affect you? Has your job been affected in any way?*
- *Are there any persons who have relevant information? Was anyone present when the alleged harassment occurred? Did you tell anyone about it? Did anyone see you immediately after episodes of alleged harassment?*
- *Did the person who harassed you harass anyone else? Do you know whether anyone complained about harassment by that person?*
- *Are there any notes, physical evidence, or other documentation regarding the incident(s)?*
- *How would you like to see the situation resolved?*
- *Do you know of any other relevant information?*

Other witnesses

Interview anyone who has knowledge that will support or deny the complainant's allegations. If possible, obtain signed statements. Witness evidence is very critical to any investigation. Without it, it is simply the complainant's word against that of the accused.

Determine whether information provided by witnesses is based on firsthand knowledge of the facts, hearsay (information or statements made by another who is not the witness—for example, a witness who says he overheard another person discussing the conduct; you'll want to interview the witness with firsthand knowledge) or gossip. And document unsuccessful attempts to interview persons who no longer work for the organization, especially if time has passed between the alleged conduct and it coming to the attention of the employer.

Be aware that often witnesses are reluctant to come forward out of fear of punishment or even of awkwardness among their fellow employees. Assure witnesses that their cooperation is important, that their testimony is confidential, and that they will not be retaliated against for providing honest responses and information. Warn witnesses of the risk of personal defamation liability if they make malicious or false statements or discuss the matter with others.

Don't unnecessarily disclose information to witnesses. For example, instead of asking, "Did you see Ramel touch Sarita?" ask "Have you seen anyone touch Sarita at work in a way that made her feel uncomfortable?"

Don't miss this! *The following are examples of EEOC approved questions that may be appropriate to ask potential witnesses:*

- *What did you see or hear? When did this occur? Describe the alleged harasser's behavior toward the complainant and toward others in the workplace.*
- *What did the complainant tell you? When did he or she tell you this?*
- *Do you know of any other relevant information?*
- *Are there other persons who have relevant information?*

✔ CHECKLIST: Interviewing the supervisor

It is critical that you interview both the complainant's and accused's supervisor(s).

☐ Ask about any discipline problems and behavior patterns on the part of either the accused or the complainant.

☐ Determine whether or not the supervisor had any knowledge of the relationship between the parties.

☐ Find out whether the complainant reported the conduct to the supervisor or if the supervisor was in a position to observe the conduct.

☐ Consider whether the supervisor should have been alerted to the conduct. For example, was the conduct discussed in the presence of the supervisor, or were there any rumors circulating?

The accused

Some experts recommend that the time to meet with the person accused of inappropriate conduct is *after* the complainant and other witnesses have been interviewed. If there is more than one person who is accused of sexual harassment, meet with each one individually rather than together.

1. Explain the reason for the meeting. Begin by telling the accused the purpose of the investigation. He or she may have no idea why the meeting was called. Provide enough information about the complaint so that the accused can know what he or she is responding to.

Explain that a full, thorough investigation of the allegations will be conducted before any conclusions are reached.

Assure the accused that confidentiality will be maintained to the fullest extent possible. Explain that disclosure of information about the complaint and investigation will be strictly limited to those with a legitimate need to know.

Don't miss this! *It is important that HR treat the accused party with respect and objectivity. Do not make assumptions about guilt based on prior history or simply on the fact that a complaint has been made. Conduct a complete investigation of the current situation.*

2. Obtain a statement. As with the complainant, ask the accused for a written statement. Interviewers often have more leverage with the accused than with the complainant because of the potential disciplinary nature of the investigation. Again, if the accused is unwilling to provide a written statement, document that fact.

3. Identify the accused's relationship to the complainant. Was the accused a supervisory employee, a coworker, or a nonemployee? If the individual was a supervisor, indicate the individual's job title, obtain a copy of the individual's job description, and determine the individual's specific duties at the time of the alleged harassment.

- Did he or she have authority to take tangible employments actions like hiring, firing, imposing discipline, or promoting?
- Was there any prior consensual relationship between the parties?
- How long have the parties known each other?
- Is there a history of group or individual socializing?
- Is there any motive for the complainant to make false charges?

4. Consider how the accused reacts. You can expect the accused to deny the charges. Observe the reaction. Note whether or not there is surprise, anger, or disbelief.

Describe the details of the complaint and pay attention to the areas of disagreement between each person's recollection of the events. If the accused denies the allegations, probe further to determine what he or she thinks are the reasons that could have motivated the employee to make the complaint. Determine if there are any facts to support the accused's side of the story.

Don't miss this! *If the person accused of harassment does not deny the conduct but explains the circumstances, there may be no need to investigate further. In this case, determine an appropriate response.*

5. Gather more evidence. Find out if there are any witnesses, documentation, or other evidence that support the accused's denial of the allegations. When faced with a "he said, she said" claim, you must investigate further. If there are no witnesses to the alleged conduct, ask other employees if they have ever been subject to objectionable conduct *but do not name the accused.* In addition to their potential liability to sexual harassment victims, employers could also be liable to harassers for inadequate or incomplete investigations. When employment decisions are going to be based on workplace sexual harassment investigations, good investigative practices must be used.

6. Caution against wrongdoing. Warn the accused that retaliation against the complainant is prohibited and can result in discipline, up to and including discharge. Caution the accused of the risk of personal defamation liability if he or she makes malicious or false statements or discusses the matter with others. It's important to stress these things in every case regardless of your personal belief as to whether or not the complaint was legitimate. Finally, assure the accused that the investigation will be impartial and thorough.

What if the accused wants a lawyer present? An alleged harasser is not entitled to attorney representation during investigatory interviews. Keep in mind, though, that the accused is probably entitled to have a union representative present if the company is unionized. Reassure the accused that:

- No conclusions have been reached;
- The investigation will be conducted fairly and objectively; and
- Confidentiality will be maintained to the fullest extent.

It is possible that the accused still might have legitimate concerns about the integrity of the process. Ask the accused to identify those concerns and take action to address them immediately.

Don't miss this! *The following are examples of EEOC-approved questions that may be appropriate to ask the accused:*

- *What is your response to the allegations?*
- *If the harasser claims that the allegations are false, ask why the complainant might lie.*
- *Are there any persons who have relevant information?*
- *Are there any notes, physical evidence, or other documentation regarding the incident(s)?*
- *Do you know of any other relevant information?*

Determining credibility

What if there are no witnesses, or the witnesses disagree? Sexual harassment often happens in private with no witnesses. The resolution of a workplace sexual harassment claim often depends upon the credibility of the parties. Unfortunately, these "he said, she said" situations may be the rule and not the exception. How do you handle a situation where it comes down to weighing two different versions of what happened? Witnesses as well may have conflicting perceptions of the same event, and their recollections can differ from those of both the complainant and the accused. So how do you determine the credibility of the information you obtain during the interview process?

★ Best practices

Although there is much information available from a variety of reputable sources on how professional investigators determine credibility, here are a few tips:

1. Watch for nonverbal cues, including facial expressions and body movements, as well as what an interviewee says. (This is one reason for having two interviewers: one can watch and listen while the other documents.)

   - As a very general rule, people who sit forward, with a relaxed body posture and arms out, are receptive to communicating freely; those who pull back, are hunched over, and have their arms crossed are signaling less willingness to communicate.

- Nodding, eye contact, smiling or looking thoughtful, open hands, and looking up, may indicate responsiveness or reflection. These tend to show a willingness to cooperate.
- Looking bored, looking down, frowning, tapping fingers or feet rapidly, clenching fists, moving backwards, or looking all around may indicate defensiveness or a lack of candor. These may show either that a witness has something to hide or is unwilling (perhaps out of fear) to cooperate.

2. Use open-ended questions and allow the interviewee to tell the story in his or her own words. This will give you a chance to follow up, probe, explore, and clarify.

3. Allow silence. Silence allows both the interviewer and interviewee an opportunity to think; it may also prompt additional information to be volunteered.

4. If information (or the witness individually) is vague, sketchy, or uses a lot of "they" or "them" pronouns, it is possible the individual is trying to direct attention away from himself or herself.

5. If a witness appears unable to recall what the interviewer believes are important details that typically would be noteworthy, this may indicate a need for follow-up, probing questions.

From "How to assess credibility in workplace investigations," Nonprofit World, Vol. 23, No.1, January/February 2005, Published by the Society for Nonprofit Organizations, https://www.snpo.org/.

State and federal agencies like the EEOC, as well as juries, can find that workplace harassment occurred based solely on the victim's description of what happened. The fact that there are no other witnesses does not automatically mean the employer should take no action. Consider the following in evaluating a "he said, she said" situation. In order to find that the victim is believable, the EEOC gives great weight to a victim's ability to provide a sufficiently detailed and internally consistent account of the events. If the employee is unable to present any facts that support his or her story, the complaint will be perceived as less believable.

> ✔ CHECKLIST: Factors to help determine whether sexual harassment occurred
>
> A general denial by the accused will carry little weight with the EEOC when other supporting evidence exists. HR should look for surrounding evidence to support or disprove a sexual harassment claim. Such evidence may be found by asking the following questions:
>
> ☐ Do coworkers have any knowledge of the conduct?
>
> ☐ Did anyone observe the victim's behavior shortly after the alleged incident of harassment? The accused's behavior?
>
> ☐ Did the victim discuss the matter with another person such as a counselor, doctor, or close friend?
>
> ☐ Did anyone notice any change in the victim's behavior at work or in the way that the alleged harasser treated the victim?
>
> ☐ Were other employees treated in a similar manner by the alleged harasser?

According to the EEOC's *Enforcement Guidance on Vicarious Employer Liability for Unlawful Harassment by Supervisors:*

Credibility assessments can be critical in determining whether the alleged harassment in fact occurred. Factors to consider include:

1. **Inherent plausibility:** Is the testimony believable on its face? Does it make sense?
2. **Demeanor:** Did the person seem to be telling the truth or lying?
3. **Motive to falsify:** Did the person have a reason to lie?
4. **Corroboration:** Is there witness testimony (such as testimony by eye-witnesses, people who saw the person soon after the alleged incidents, or people who discussed the incidents with him or her at around the time that they occurred) or physical evidence (such as written documentation) that corroborates the party's testimony?
5. **Past record:** Did the alleged harasser have a history of similar behavior in the past?

None of the above factors are determinative as to credibility. For example, the fact that there are no eye-witnesses to the alleged harassment by no means necessarily defeats the complainant's credibility, since harassment often occurs behind closed doors. Furthermore, the fact that the alleged harasser engaged in similar behavior in the past does not necessarily mean that he or she did so again.

> **Don't miss this!** E. Jason Tremblay, an attorney with Arnstein & Lehr LLP, suggests a word of caution. He points out that "great care is required to be sure that the investigation does not produce admissions against interest and a road map to easy victory for a plaintiff's attorney. In order to minimize such risks, the investigator should limit questions to requests for factual information only, writing only verified factual details while steering away from recording mental impressions, conclusions, or speculation, particularly ones having the effect of suggesting fault or liability on behalf of the company or its agents."

Documenting the process

A complete and accurate record can show that an employer promptly and thoroughly investigated a sexual harassment complaint and that its resolution of the complaint was appropriate. Also, it can be invaluable in defending against a wrongful discharge or defamation lawsuit by a person found to have engaged in inappropriate harassing conduct.

Therefore, it is critical that investigators develop and retain accurate records of the particulars of a workplace harassment investigation.

- Take detailed notes during all interviews (another reason to have two interviewers).
- Save all written statements submitted by the complainant, the accused, and witnesses, as well as any other documentation or materials acquired during the investigation.
- Do not attempt to reach a legal conclusion in the documentation, but refer to violations of the employer's policy.
  - For example, don't say that William sexually harassed Margo. Instead, say that William repeatedly asked Margo to date him over her stated objections, repeatedly made sexual comments to Margo, and repeatedly complained about his marital relations to Margo, again over her objections.
- Once you have specified the factual information that you gathered, you can then categorize it as inappropriate or unprofessional conduct according to your employer's policy.

Don't miss this! Preserve the complete record in a safe, confidential manner for at least as long as may be required by any applicable regulatory or state statute of limitations—this means years, not months. The records may also help the employer identify patterns of harassment that could assist in improving preventive measures, including training.

Maintaining confidentiality

Once an investigation begins, keep the facts as confidential as possible and reveal them only on a strict "need to know" basis. Don't promise complete confidentiality, either in the sexual harassment policy or during the investigation's interviews. Employers cannot promise the complaining employee that his or her identity will not ever be revealed. To fairly confront the alleged harasser, legal experts advise that the investigator must be able to say who complained or what the objectionable conduct was.

Everyone involved in the investigation—including the person making the report, the accused, and witnesses—should be informed that the employer will keep the investigation as confidential as circumstances permit. Making sure that workplace sexual harassment complaints and investigations are handled as confidentially as possible by the employer not only will encourage employees to come forward with their complaints, but will also reduce the risk of a defamation lawsuit.

Don't miss this! There is tension between the EEOC's recommendation that employers require participants in a disciplinary investigation—like a sexual harassment investigation—to keep it confidential and the National Labor Relations Board's position that employees have a right to share employment-related information with each other under federal labor law. In a noteworthy federal court of appeals decision from 2017, the appeals court found that a health system's confidentiality agreement that restricted employees from discussing ongoing disciplinary investigations involving themselves or coworkers was not lawful, but the employer's investigative nondisclosure policy was lawful because there was no evidence that employees were categorically required, in all HR investigations involving certain types of misconduct, to keep information confidential.

Employer policies. All new hires were required to sign a confidentiality agreement that defined "confidential information" to include "private employee information (such as salaries, disciplinary action, etc.) that is not shared by the employee." It also stated that "keeping this kind of information private and confidential is so important that if I fail to do so, I understand that I could be subject to corrective action, including termination and possibly legal action." The court found this unlawful.

The nondisclosure policy was contained in an "interview of complainant" form that the employer relied upon when investigating complaints. The "Introduction for all interviews" section included the statement: "I ask you not to discuss this with your coworkers while this investigation is going on, for this reason, when people are talking it is difficult to do a fair investigation and separate facts from rumors." However, employees were never given a copy of the form and nondisclosure was not requested routinely, except only "in the more sensitive situations, like sexual harassment and suspicion of abuse." The court did not agree that this approach—given that it wasn't applied to every investigation—unlawfully interfered with employee labor rights.

In recognition of this tension and the untenable situation it can put employers in, the EEOC has recommended that the agency and the National Labor Relations Board "should confer, consult, and attempt to jointly clarify and harmonize the interplay of the National Labor Relations Act and federal EEO statutes with regard to the permissible confidentiality of workplace investigations."

Stay tuned.

Understanding and avoiding defamation

What is defamation? Defamation involves a false or malicious (intentionally harmful) statement, either written or spoken, about another that results in damage to that person's reputation. Not only can an employer be faced with defamation liability based on statements made in connection with the investigation or resolution of a sexual harassment complaint, so can the individuals who made the statements.

Truth is an absolute defense to defamation claims, but there is always the risk that either the complaint or statements made during an investigation are false or exaggerated, or even that a finding of harassment is actually mistaken. Moreover, while a "qualified privilege" may protect investigators and witnesses who make defamatory statements, the privilege will be lost if the statements are recklessly or maliciously made, if they go beyond the scope of the investigation, or if they are made to someone who has no legitimate need to know about the matter.

> ✔ **CHECKLIST: Preventing defamation during a sexual harassment investigation**
>
> Follow these tips to avoid the risk of defamation liability:
>
> ☐ Never discuss a workplace sexual harassment complaint with any-one who does not have a legitimate need to receive the information.
> ☐ Make sure that all discussions of the matter are in a private area and cannot be overheard.
> ☐ Do not send email or texts, or leave voice mail, that disclose details of a workplace sexual harassment complaint or investigation.
> ☐ Do not seek information or make statements concerning the parties that go beyond the scope of the investigation.
> ☐ Caution the accused, accuser, and witnesses about their risk of personal defamation liability if they make spiteful or untrue statements during an investigation or discuss the matter with others.
> ☐ Do not draw any conclusions about the matter before all the facts are received and reviewed.
> ☐ Develop a complete and accurate written record of all investigative interviews. When possible, obtain written statements.
> ☐ Make sure that the final determination is based solidly on the facts. Never describe the conduct as worse than it was.
> ☐ Keep confidential all records concerning a sexual harassment investigation. Records should be kept in a separate confidential file, not in the accused's personnel file (in most instances; you may need to check your state's laws).
> ☐ Do not broadcast the results of the investigation as an example to others or as a training tool.
> ☐ If the investigation determines that a complaint has merit, do not refer to the harasser's conduct as "sexual harassment." Rather, refer to it as "unprofessional" or "inappropriate" conduct. That way, if there is a policy against inappropriate conduct in place (and there should be), the employer may take necessary disciplinary action and still avoid the battle of determining whether the behavior at issue amounts to a legal definition of sexual harassment.

Protecting the accuser and the accused during the investigation

Depending on how severe the alleged harassment is, it may be necessary to take corrective action *during* the investigation. Doing so can serve to reduce the risk that the complainant will quit and/or take legal action, as well as help prevent liability if a lawsuit is filed.

> ### ✔ CHECKLIST: Remedies for harassment during an investigation
>
> Possible corrective actions include:
>
> - ☐ Immediate removal of offensive graffiti or materials (photographs, cartoons, etc.) from the workplace.
> - ☐ Making scheduling changes to avoid contact between the parties.
> - ☐ Temporarily transferring either the alleged harasser or the complainant (but heed the cautionary note below).
> - ☐ Offering the complainant a paid leave of absence.
> - ☐ Offering to pay for counseling for the complainant.
> - ☐ Placing the alleged harasser on a nondisciplinary leave of absence.

Any job transfer during the investigation—of the complainant or the accused—must not disadvantage either party. Any perception that the reassignment is "less than" the current assignment can be interpreted as retaliation. It is generally a good idea to make reassignment offers dependent upon the approval of those involved. However, it is not required that corrective measures be those that the employee requests or prefers. What matters is that they are effective.

Chapter 7

Resolution and corrective action

Blythe, an employee in your organization, has made a complaint to the HR office stating she has been the victim of sexual harassment. As part of your investigation, you reviewed relevant documents and interviewed Blythe and Colin, the coworker she accused of harassment. In addition, you interviewed their supervisor, Kathryn, and the other coworker in the group, Juanita.

Blythe looked directly at you, spoke quietly, and gave a detailed description of her side of the story. But Colin adamantly denied that he did anything Blythe didn't welcome. He admitted he made sexually suggestive jokes, but claimed that Blythe never complained and always laughed at them. He said it was all in good fun and he had no idea Blythe was offended. Kathryn had no knowledge of any inappropriate jokes or comments by Colin—to Blythe or anyone else in the workplace. She noticed, though, that Blythe had been "keeping to herself" and had been taking a lot of time off lately.

Juanita recalled several times when Colin "teased" Blythe about her sex life and bragged about his, told raunchy jokes, and one time taped a sexually explicit cartoon on Blythe's desk. According to Juanita, when Blythe saw the carton, she walked away and didn't return to the work area for several minutes. What should your organization do now?

Making a determination

Once the employer has thoroughly investigated potential sexual harassment it must determine:

1. Whether a violation of the sexual harassment policy occurred, and
2. What action to take based on the investigation's findings.

Whatever the final determination, it must be well founded and solidly supported by facts in the investigative record. Because the decision about what to do may not completely satisfy the complaining employee, it is important the employee understand that the employer is taking the *appropriate* steps.

✔ CHECKLIST: Counseling the complaining employee

To help the employee accept the results of the investigation and the employer's decision, an employer should take the following actions, some even before the decision is communicated:

☐ Provide someone sympathetic and credible to whom the employee can talk.

☐ Help the employee understand what is and is not sexual harassment as defined by law and the employer's policy.

☐ Explain how and why the employer has made the determination it has and what it hopes to accomplish.

☐ Make sure the employee feels secure about the immediate future.

☐ Determine whether the employee fears further harassment or retaliation, and if so, explain what he or she should do about it given the situation.

The hard-to-resolve claim

Even if the employer does everything right, it may still be impossible to determine whether sexual harassment has occurred. An organization may have a strong policy against harassment. It may conduct sexual harassment training. An effective complaint procedure may be in place. Yet, when it receives a complaint, conflicting and ambiguous evidence can make it impossible to determine exactly what happened.

This happens most often in "he said, she said" situations. For instance, the target of the claimed harassment might make a complaint like this about a coworker: "He made off-color jokes I was supposed to laugh at, stared provocatively at me, and brushed himself against me on several occasions."

When the accused harasser is questioned during the investigation, however, he may declare with great certainty and apparent honesty, "Yes, I made off-color jokes, but I was careful. I watched to see how she was taking them, and she always seemed to smile. But that's all I did; I never stared at her, and I certainly didn't brush myself against her."

What does the employer confront in a case like this? If both employees stick to their stories—"He harassed me" and "No, I didn't"—and there are no witnesses or other corroborating evidence, the investigation may never reveal what actually occurred.

Bring closure. Still, the employer must bring the complaint to some formal conclusion through investigation and continued communication with all parties involved. The steps in the process and the final resolution should be documented, as with every other aspect of the investigation.

At the very least, employers should:

- Document that a complaint was received and an investigation took place, but that it could not be determined if inappropriate conduct actually occurred.
- Explain to the employee that his or her allegations could not be substantiated.
- Thank the employee for coming forward and reassure the employee that his or her employment conditions will not be adversely affected by making the complaint.
- Urge the employee to immediately report any future incidents that he or she believes violate the employer's policies.
- Remind the alleged harasser that the organization has a policy prohibiting sexual harassment and explain the penalties for violating it.

> **Don't miss this!** *If the complaint can't be proven either way, do not discipline either the alleged harasser or the victim. The employer, however, should still consider preventive measures such as counseling, training, or monitoring.*

Of course, there is no guarantee that the target who perceived harassment will not take the complaint elsewhere—such as to a lawyer or even to the EEOC. But taking steps to resolve the complaint will put the employer in a much better position to explain the organization's position should it be required to defend its actions.

Taking prompt action

If it is determined that sexual harassment did occur, an employer must take prompt corrective action to stop the behavior.

✔ CHECKLIST: Types of corrective action

- ☐ An apology for an unintentionally offensive remark.
- ☐ Disciplinary action that reflects the severity of the conduct and that might include a warning, reprimand, suspension, or even discharge.
- ☐ Training for the accused about the inappropriate behavior and the employer's sexual harassment policy.
- ☐ Monitoring of the accused to be certain the harassment stops.
- ☐ Restoring any job benefits or opportunities to the target that were lost because of the harassment.
- ☐ Counseling or other compensation for losses.
- ☐ Expunging any negative evaluations in the employee's personnel file that arose from the harassment.
- ☐ Additional training for the workforce about inappropriate workplace behavior.

Don't miss this! Corrective action, according to the EEOC, should be proportionate to the seriousness of the offense. If the harassment was minor, such as a small number of "off-color" remarks by an individual with no prior history of similar misconduct, then counseling and an oral warning might be all that is necessary. On the other hand, if the harassment was severe or persistent despite prior corrective action, then suspension or discharge may be appropriate.

Restoration is the goal. The actions taken should be designed to correct the behavior and to prevent it from happening again. The overall goal should be to place the employee who complained in the position that he or she would have been in if the misconduct had never occurred.

Example: Felicia, a corrections officer at a federal prison, claimed Larry, a male coworker, inappropriately hugged her and made sexual comments, including references to her "juicy thighs." On the same day he allegedly slapped her on the buttocks twice, she filed a formal complaint about that incident. The company then told Larry to stay away from Felicia. In the days after her complaint, he rolled his eyes at her once and punched a metal machine in her presence, allegedly to intimidate her. She complained a second time. However, he never touched her or made inappropriate comments after her first complaint.

The company brought in an outside investigator to look at these and other complaints against Larry. In an interview, Felicia then described two prior incidents of alleged inappropriate hugging and sexual comments. Two months after the first complaint, the investigator submitted a report finding Larry had sexually harassed Felicia and other coworkers. Larry was fired days later.

Felicia still sued her employer for sexual harassment. Although a jury returned a verdict for Felicia, awarding her $4,000 in actual damages and $100,000 in punitive damages, a federal court found that the employer's prompt remedial action in response to Felicia's complaints kept it from being held legally responsible. There was no evidence supporting Felicia's claim her employer should have known about the sexual harassment before her first complaint that her coworker had slapped her on the buttocks. It was not until the date of the investigator's report that the organization knew of two prior occasions of inappropriate touching and comments.

Although Felicia argued the employer should have known of Larry's inappropriate habit of hugging female employees, she testified that she never reported the hugging, and there was no evidence the hugging was widespread or that other employees considered it offensive. Nor did Felicia report Larry's intimidating conduct, and there was no evidence to show the employer should have known about it at the time.

Employer enforced policy. Even assuming that the employer had constructive knowledge of the harassment, it was insulated from liability based on its comprehensive, well-known anti-discrimination policy. While Felicia claimed it wasn't vigorously enforced, Larry was admonished, investigated, and then terminated.

Effective and prompt. *Because the employer's actions prevented a recurrence of harassment about which it knew, it took remedial action that was effective. As for whether it was sufficiently prompt, the employer immediately ordered Larry to avoid contact with Felicia and then fired him after the investigator's report. And while Felicia argued that six weeks between her first complaint and the investigator's interview was too long, the court noted that there were a "lot of moving parts in the company's investigation, and each of those workings took time." For example, both of Felicia's written complaints had to be examined internally and referred to the ethics office, other employees' allegations had to be investigated, and another investigator had to be brought in from out of state; she interviewed 16 employees. In light of all of this, the company acted promptly, and it avoided legal liability.*

Consider Blythe's situation. It appears that Colin did make lewd jokes and comments to Blythe. While his behavior may or may not violate federal law, it is inappropriate and must be stopped. Colin should be disciplined and monitored to make sure his behavior does not continue. Sexual harassment training is surely in order, at least for Colin; possibly for the entire workforce.

Consider also bystander intervention training to help employees like Juanita, who witnessed Colin's behavior, understand how to intervene in a situation to stop the inappropriate conduct.

To help Blythe return to a comfortable work environment, the employer should consider offering counseling services. It may also be necessary to compensate her for any unpaid time she took away from work due to stress caused by the inappropriate behavior.

★ Best practices

Supervisor reports harassment. Not long after she was hired as a catering manager for a community college system, Nadia claimed that Jose began sexually harassing her. When Emma, Jose's supervisor, heard there was tension between the two employees, she called Nadia, who told her Jose had been making advances that made her uncomfortable. Emma encouraged Nadia to file a complaint with the EEO office, but Nadia did not want to cause trouble. Nonetheless, Emma reported the issue to HR.

Insufficient evidence. Emma also told Jose he was not to be alone with Nadia or "treat her in a way that would be considered problematic." Despite this, Nadia claimed that things got worse and that Jose and his friend began to "throw her under the bus." When she asked Emma to come and see what was going on, Emma again told Nadia to follow up with the EEO office. Nadia subsequently filed a written EEO complaint against Jose but an investigation found insufficient evidence of sexual harassment.

Termination. Around a month later, Emma recommended that Nadia be terminated based on reports of unprofessional behavior that included "drinking during an event that she was managing, ... telling our clients that we're not capable of managing our events, behavior leading to stress with our landlord, among ... a list of smaller things that were going on as well."

EEO complaint stops harassment. Although Nadia sued, alleging sexual harassment, a court found her employer was not liable. Emma, upon hearing of the tension between Nadia and Jose, reached out to Nadia on her own initiative to inquire about their relationship. She then told Nadia to file an EEO complaint and also immediately notified HR, which led to HR sending a letter and a copy of the EEO complaint form to Nadia that same day. Further, when Nadia complained that Jose and his friend were "giving her grief," Emma reiterated that she should follow up with the EEO office. When Nadia finally did file a complaint, the harassment stopped.

Rejecting Nadia's suggestion that her employer should have taken additional actions such as disciplining Jose or trying harder to separate them, the court pointed out that "it was apparently the mere threat of an imminent EEO investigation that stopped the harassment from recurring, and the cessation of the harassment shows the effectiveness of the corrective action."

Not self-enforcing. And while Nadia argued that her employer failed to take corrective action promptly enough, as Emma knew the harassment continued for two weeks after Nadia first complained and before she filed her complaint, the court, observing that "the law against sexual harassment is not self-enforcing," pointed out that Nadia admitted *she* delayed submitting a written complaint (although she received a written complaint form from the EEO office) and that she was repeatedly told to submit a written complaint.

Notice of resolution

Once the investigation has been completed, those who were involved should be told the results of the investigation and whether or not corrective action was taken. But how much should you reveal?

Don't miss this! *Attorney Chris Bourgeacq, the Chris Bourgeacq Law Firm, does not recommend giving much detail to the victim about what was done to the accused party. "There's no legal duty to provide that information. Sometimes the action is obvious—when the harasser is fired, for example. Other times, the harasser may be disciplined in ways about which other employees do not have a need to know. Telling the victim only that the matter was investigated, substantiated, and steps were taken to prevent it from occurring again is typically the better approach."*

Addressing the victim

Once an employer determines that sexual harassment or other inappropriate behavior occurred, it must also take action that will ensure that the victim is no longer subject to the wrongful behavior.

Depending on the circumstances, it may be enough to counsel the harasser and arrange for an apology. Or, if the conduct was more severe, the organization may need to arrange for a transfer or reassignment. In some cases it may be appropriate to offer counseling services to overcome the stress caused by the harassment. This may be a good time to offer the company's EAP services, if available.

Example: *An employee filed a formal complaint because her manager called her "honey" once in five years. The employer investigated, interviewing employees, including another manager who was present and who believed that the use of "honey" sounded more colloquial than sexual. Observing that saying "honey" in this context is not severe enough to be actionable, attorney Chris Bourgeacq explained that at most, some low-key counseling to the manager/management team reminding them of different perceptions and the potential for harassment claims likely would suffice.*

HR must also address the victim's needs by restoring any job benefits or opportunities that may have been lost because of the harassment. This may include compensation for any lost pay or sick days used because of the stress of the harassment. It may also be necessary for HR to expunge negative comments from a performance review tainted by a harassing supervisor's motives.

Transfers and reassignments

In some cases it may be appropriate to separate the victim and the harasser. Exercise extreme caution in this area. Any transfer must not appear to disadvantage the person making the harassment complaint. If the complaining employee is reassigned, for example, to a less desirable position or to a position with few promotion opportunities, this may be seen as retaliating against the employee for making a complaint.

- When attempting to remedy sexual harassment, avoid requiring that the complaining employee work less desirable hours or in a less desirable location.
- If HR offers to transfer the complaining employee, try first to obtain his or her consent, and make sure the new position is substantially similar to his or her prior position.

Worst case scenario

A federal appeals court found ample evidence to support a jury's determination that a state police department was legally responsible for the retaliatory acts of a female police sergeant's supervisor, who responded to the sergeant's second complaint of coworker sexual harassment by asking his superior and the HR department to transfer the sergeant (not the harasser) because her complaints were creating a hostile work environment. Transferring the alleged harasser was never considered.

Affirming the jury's $350,000 award to the sergeant, the court noted that the supervisor also had a hand in the hearing that determined where the sergeant's new assignment would be, which was 180 miles from her home!

The false complaint

What if the sexual harassment allegations turn out to be false? It is important for HR to determine whether the individual who complained deliberately lied or simply misperceived the conduct. Disciplining someone who mistakenly reported harassment not only can discourage other employees from making complaints, but it also can result in liability for retaliation.

Don't impose discipline on the complaining party unless you are absolutely certain the person was fully aware of the falsity of the claim at the time it was made. If discipline is warranted, it should be consistent with the discipline your organization otherwise would impose for dishonesty in comparable circumstances.

> **Don't miss this!** *When asked how to handle a situation where an employee makes repeated, unsubstantiated allegations against a coworker, attorney Chris Bourgeacq noted that while retaliating against someone for opposing discrimination is prohibited by law, it's a good idea to include in a harassment policy or employee handbook that making false accusations against an employee is misconduct that can lead to discipline, including termination.*

Disciplining the offender

If harassment is found, the employer must decide how to appropriately discipline the harasser. When imposing discipline, consider the severity, past history, frequency, and pervasiveness of the conduct.

Appropriate forms of discipline can include oral or written warnings, reprimands, demotion, suspension, and probation. If the conduct is very offensive or if the harasser's ability to perform is very impaired, discharge may be the only alternative. Lesser discipline should be accompanied with a warning that any similar misconduct in the future will result in immediate discharge.

Also, consider any imbalance of power between the target and the harasser. A supervisory/subordinate relationship, for example, or other situation where it is apparent that the harasser held significantly more organizational power than his or her target may warrant more substantial disciplinary action to account for the abuse of power.

Worst case scenario

Harassment starts immediately. Audrey, a female production worker, alleged she was sexually harassed by Caden, her coworker. She claimed that on his first day of work, he made sexually explicit comments to her and rubbed the side of her breast. Although Audrey reported the incident to a Team Lead, he did not report it to anyone else. The next day, Caden made more explicit comments, told Audrey that he gave another coworker some nude photographs to show her, invaded her personal space, and acted jealous whenever she spoke with another male employee. She again complained, but Caden's behavior continued, and the coworker who was given the nude photos actually showed them to Audrey.

Disciplinary action. Audrey reported Caden's conduct to a manager at the beginning of her next shift, and HR was alerted. Caden was suspended without pay for one day for distributing the nude photos. When he returned, HR issued him a pre-termination warning and reviewed its sexual harassment policy with him. Afterward, Caden stared at Audrey in a way that made her feel uncomfortable, so she reported the incident to HR. Within two weeks, the employer moved Caden to a different department and conducted facility-wide training on its sexual harassment policy. However, Caden continued to intimidate Audrey whenever he came to her work area.

EEOC charges. Audrey claimed that after she reported Caden's conduct, the HR manager berated her for reporting him and threatened to write her up or fire her. Audrey filed an EEOC charge; eight days later, a manager reprimanded her for a work error.

Audrey then filed a second EEOC charge alleging retaliation for reporting sexual harassment. Sometime later, Caden came to Audrey's work area and walked circles around her. On another occasion, he rubbed her shoulders without her consent. Audrey eventually sued, alleging a sexually hostile work environment and retaliation.

Was employer's response to harassment "reasonable?" In a case with similar facts, a federal court rejected the employer's assertion that its response to Caden's harassment was "reasonable." Although there was evidence that its actions were reasonable (such as its facility-wide training on its sexual harassment policy), there was also evidence that at times it did not respond reasonably to Audrey's allegations. For instance, it suspended Caden for distributing nude photos, not for harassing Audrey. And while it issued Caden a written warning, the warning did not reference any of the specific acts of harassment, only the photos.

Was transfer reasonable? Nor was transferring Caden necessarily a reasonable response, as the employer never told him why it moved him from Audrey's work area, and Caden had already requested the transfer *because it paid more.* Audrey had also asked for a transfer to resolve the issue, but HR told her that the only available position paid less than she was earning. It would be up to a jury to decide whether offering Caden a higher-paying job while offering Audrey a lower-paying one was reasonable.

Additionally, the adequacy of the HR manager's response was at issue, as she did not interview a witness to the harassment, never spoke with Audrey about her allegations concerning Caden's sexually explicit comments, and drafted the official report of the harassment over a month after Audrey lodged her complaint.

Don't miss this! Employers, notes the EEOC, have a heightened responsibility to protect employees against abuse of official power. To that end, employers must take steps to prevent employees who have been granted authority over others from using it to further harassment, even if that authority is insufficient to establish vicarious liability. Thus, the nature and degree of the harasser's authority should be considered in evaluating the adequacy of corrective action.

★ Best practices

Postal Service picks suitable discipline for questionable conduct

The U.S. Postal Service avoided liability for sexual harassment because it took appropriate corrective action by disciplining a male coworker found to have sexually harassed a female employee. The Postal Service learned of the alleged harasser's questionable conduct when another employee reported having seen the accused grab the female employee's hand with the intention of kissing it and refusing to let go—despite her protests. Management investigated within three days of the report, and the accused's supervisor reprimanded him and warned him on two occasions to stay away from the female employee. Because the employee found the male employee's presence discomfiting, management also moved her to a different job farther away from his area.

The victim argued to a court that the Postal Service should have disciplined the male employee more extensively. But the court disagreed. It viewed the admonishments as adequate discipline given that there were 16 reported incidents of harassing behavior, none of which were severe and pervasive enough to create a hostile working environment. The discipline imposed, along with the removal of the female employee from the work area, stopped the harassment altogether; that showed that it was sufficient.

Be consistent

Ensure that all employer actions taken for violating the sexual harassment and inappropriate behavior policy are not only timely, but also consistent. Sometimes employees who have been disciplined or terminated for sexual harassment will later claim they instead were unlawfully discriminated against because of their sex, race, age, or other protected characteristic. In other words, they say that they were treated differently from other employees accused of inappropriate workplace behavior.

Therefore, before disciplining or discharging an employee accused of sexual harassment, carefully consider how the organization has treated other workers accused of similar behavior. To assist with this review, HR should maintain confidential records regarding harassment investigations and claims.

Addressing the workforce

HR may need to take additional corrective action that will persuade potential harassers to refrain from unlawful sexual harassment. Some actions that may be taken include:

- Conduct refresher anti-harassment training for all employees and supervisory personnel.
- Establish front-line recognition of what sexual harassment is. Use specific examples; highlight areas of behavior that are not so easy to characterize; elaborate so that the message is clear.
- Eliminate a culture that encourages sexual harassment. Starting with the very top executives in your organization, discourage swearing, off-color jokes, crude humor, gender bias, and after-work socializing that includes heavy drinking. Emphasize the importance of setting the same high standard of behavior even outside of the workplace, such as during business trips. Include conformity with these standards in individual managers' annual performance goals.
- Redistribute the sexual harassment policy. Make sure the policy contains all necessary elements, including effective complaint procedures.

Preventing retaliation

Just as an employer must promptly and effectively stop sexual harassment, it must do the same with respect to retaliatory activity. Some of the most obvious types of unlawful retaliation are denial of a promotion or job benefits, demotion, suspension, and discharge. Retaliation may also take the form of threats, reprimands, negative evaluations, and harassment.

Failure to stop retaliation against an employee who complains of sexual harassment, or someone who participates in a harassment investigation, can result in legal liability for an employer, regardless of the outcome of the investigation. An employer can be held responsible not only for retaliatory actions by managers and supervisors but also for those by coworkers.

Example: *An employer and its affiliate agreed to pay $850,000 to eight former and current employees to settle allegations that the companies had unlawfully permitted female janitors to be sexually harassed and retaliated against managers who supported the janitors' sexual harassment claims. Six female janitors assigned to work the night shift at a federal building allegedly faced routine sexual harassment by their direct supervisor, according to the EEOC, which claimed that two managers were unfairly criticized and disciplined in retaliation for supporting the women's sexual harassment claims—including assisting them in filing complaints with the EEOC—and that one manager was compelled to resign.*

In addition to the monetary relief the employers had to pay, the court-approved consent decree required the employers to revise their EEO policies and complaint and investigation procedures; institute supervisor accountability policies concerning discrimination issues; conduct comprehensive workforce training; hire a consultant to monitor any responses to future complaints; and provide reports to the EEOC on compliance with the decree's terms.

Observed an EEOC district director: "The #MeToo movement illustrates that sexual harassment impacts people across industries, from white collar to blue collar work, across class, race, age, gender, and abilities. In this case, there were many factors that contributed to the vulnerability of these janitors—all were African-American, many were young females new to the workplace, with disabilities, working the isolated night shift. Employers must take proactive measures to stop predators who would abuse their power over vulnerable workers."

Don't miss this! Unlawful retaliation can occur even after the employment relationship ends. For example, a negative job reference may be viewed by a court as retaliatory if the reason the bad reference was provided was to "punish" the worker for having participated in an EEOC investigation.

✔ CHECKLIST: Steps for addressing retaliation

Employers should anticipate, prevent, and respond to possible retaliation by:

- ☐ Encouraging the person who reported sexual harassment, as well as workers who participate in the investigation, to let HR or a member of management know immediately if the behavior continues or if there are any further problems.

- ☐ Monitoring the situation in order to ensure that the alleged harasser does not engage in retaliatory or other inappropriate conduct.

- ☐ Stopping—immediately—any conduct that appears to be retaliatory.

- ☐ Counseling employees suspected or accused of retaliation about what retaliation is and the consequences for engaging in such action.

- ☐ Following up to ensure retaliation does not resume.

Typically, very severe penalties including discharge are applied to individuals who retaliate, especially after having been warned not to do so in the course of an investigation. Additional corrective actions should be considered, such as meetings, statements, and training focusing on retaliation and the employer's strict prohibition against it.

Documenting the process

It is crucial that an employer make a record of what was said during the investigation and what was done in response. Documentation is important to ensure that, down the road, other individuals with a need to know are able to acquire knowledge of the investigation—if additional accusations are made or if a similar situation arises in which it is important for the employer to act consistently.

Documentation is also important in case an EEOC charge or lawsuit is brought against the organization. The employer's documents are often at the heart of such disputes.

> ***Don't miss this!*** *Keeping records of complaints also allows HR to review for possible patterns of sexual harassment by the same individual.*

Document facts, not conclusions. Characterizations, adjectives, and adverbs should be used sparingly, if at all, in your documentation. The goal is to document what people have actually said or done. For example, don't document that "Raj said Marissa was upset by Steve's crude behavior." Instead record that "Raj heard Steve tell Marissa he liked her because she reminded him of a stripper and he asked her to stand up so he could 'wand' her with a metal detector" and that "within a few minutes of hearing this comment, Raj saw Marissa begin to cry and leave the room."

Documentation of the investigative process should not be placed in either the harasser or the harassed employee's personnel files, unless or until it is determined that inappropriate conduct occurred and that discipline is necessary. Be sure to check your state's legal requirements.

Following up

Follow-up is necessary to make sure that the remedy the organization has imposed has been effective to stop the harassment and that no retaliation has been taken against the victim or witnesses. If the remedy has been ineffective, it may be necessary to increase the level of discipline. An employer's failure to follow up can result in liability if harassment continues.

> ***Don't miss this!*** *Whether the harassment stopped as a result of the corrective action is a key factor in determining whether the corrective action was appropriate, says the EEOC. The continuation of harassment despite an employer's appropriate corrective action does not necessarily mean, however, that the corrective action was inadequate.*
>
> *For example, if an employer takes appropriate, proportionate corrective action against a first-time offender who engaged in mildly offensive sexual conduct, yet the same employee subsequently engaged in further harassment, then the employer would not be liable if it also responded appropriately to the subsequent misconduct by escalating its corrective action. Conversely, where an employer undertakes no action in response to a complaint of harassment, the fact that the harassment "fortuitously stops" does not shield it from liability.*

Worst case scenario

After Joyce's first complaint of sexual harassment by Karl, a male cowork-er, management investigated and then told Karl his conduct must stop. He was warned that discipline would result if the conduct resumed. But Joyce subsequently reported repeated instances of harassment by Karl. Management responded by adjusting the employees' shifts to reduce contact between them and by counseling Karl and issuing additional oral warnings to him. Still, the harassment continued. Karl was never reprimanded, issued a written warning, or disciplined in any manner. Joyce took her claim to court and won. The court said that although management took corrective action, the employer was still liable be-cause its actions were not reasonably designed to end the harassment.

HR must follow up to make sure that the sexual harassment stops or the employer will face legal liability if the behavior continues. If a lesser de-gree of discipline has been ineffective, it may be necessary to take more severe measures to end the harassment.

Use of nondisclosure agreements

It is not unusual for employers to use nondisclosure agreements in settling any employment-related claims, including sexual harassment claims. The nondisclosure agreement—a contract between the complaining employee and the employer in which one or both agree not to disclose certain informa-tion, such as the amount of the settlement or the allegations involved in the claim—may be used to settle a sexual harassment claim for many reasons, including to resolve claims where it is unclear whether the alleged conduct occurred, to avoid incurring large legal fees, or to keep particularly salacious accusations from becoming public.

Preventing transparency? Although commonly used in many different types of settlement agreements, since the rise of the #MeToo movement, the use of these agreements in sexual harassment claims has been criticized as a way of preventing transparency and allowing sexual harassment in the workplace to continue unchecked. For example, in many of the high-profile cases that came to light as a result of the #MeToo movement, serial harassers remained in place due in large part to nondisclosure agreements that prevented other potential victims—and the public—from knowing about the problem.

Many believe these agreements should be barred, but observes Sherman and Howard attorney Brooke Colaizzi, a prohibition on nondisclosure agreements may or may not help the sexual harassment problem in the workplace. "It certainly might encourage more diligence in policy enforcement. It also may encourage employers to take swift action when an allegation is made. However, it may encourage them to take swift action without a thorough investigation process because if allegations could become public at any time employers will want their remedies to look responsive and attractive."

In addition, not only have some states started taking action to ban the use of nondisclosure agreements in the sexual harassment context, the federal Tax Cuts and Jobs Act, passed in 2017, includes a provision aimed at curbing their use in sexual harassment cases by barring employers from deducting any settlement or payment related to sexual harassment if the settlement or payment is subject to a nondisclosure agreement, or attorneys' fees are related to a settlement or payment.

This language, notes attorney Chris Bourgeacq, "may arguably discourage employers' use of nondisclosure agreements, assuming employers are even aware of the prohibition." The question employers will face is a matter of "balancing the impact of publicity about the settlement versus the economic benefit of having or losing the deductions at issue. That analysis will likely apply on a case-by-case basis."

Corrective action and the corporate culture

Of course, preventing sexual harassment in the first place is the ultimate goal. The cornerstone of a successful harassment prevention strategy, notes the EEOC in its 2018 unpublished guidance, is the consistent and demonstrated commitment of senior leaders to create and maintain a culture of respect in which harassment is not tolerated.

A June 2018 nationwide study on workplace sexual harassment by the National Academies of Sciences, Engineering, and Medicine found that "Organizational climate is the single most important factor in determining whether sexual harassment is likely to occur in a work setting." In order to prevent sexual harassment, the report concluded, system-wide changes are needed to the organizational climate.

Organizational commitment. The report, which focused on sexual harassment in the academic setting, listed six approaches that can improve the organizational climate. These approaches, it stated, "are what an organization committed to significantly reducing or eliminating sexual harassment in academia should work on implementing:

- Create a diverse, inclusive, and respectful environment;
- Diffuse the power structure and reduce isolation;
- Develop supportive structures and systems for those who experience sexual harassment;
- Improve transparency and accountability;
- Ensure there is diverse, effective, and accountable leadership that is unambiguous about its commitment to reducing and eliminating harassment; and
- Develop and use effective sexual harassment training."

Key predictor. The report noted that one of the key predictors of sexual harassment is a male-dominated organizational context. "Male-dominated organizational contexts are those settings that are numerically male dominated, have mostly men in authority roles, and/or have women working in traditionally male fields, and it is these settings that tend to have higher rates of sexual harassment. Two important steps in correcting this problem are achieving critical masses of women at every level, and changing policies and practices that are impeding the ability for women to enter and advance."

Compliance is not enough. The EEOC's Select Task Force found that "To achieve a workplace without harassment, the values of the organization must put a premium on diversity and inclusion, must include a belief that all employees in a workplace deserve to be respected, regardless of their race, religion, national origin, sex (including pregnancy, sexual orientation, or gender identity), age, disability, or genetic information, and must make clear that part of respect means not harassing an individual on any of those bases. In short, an organization's commitment to a harassment-free workplace must not be based on a compliance mindset, and instead must be part of an overall diversity and inclusion strategy."

The Task Force recommends that:

- Employers should foster an organizational culture in which harassment is not tolerated, and in which respect and civility are promoted. Employers should communicate and model a consistent commitment to that goal.
- Employers should assess their workplaces for the risk factors associated with harassment and explore ideas for minimizing those risks.
- Employers should conduct climate surveys to assess the extent to which harassment is a problem in their organization.

- Employers should devote sufficient resources to harassment prevention efforts, both to ensure that such efforts are effective, and to reinforce the credibility of leadership's commitment to creating a workplace free of harassment.
- Employers should ensure that where harassment is found to have occurred, discipline is prompt and proportionate to the severity of the infraction. In addition, employers should ensure that where harassment is found to have occurred, discipline is consistent, and does not give (or create the appearance of) undue favor to any particular employee.
- Employers should hold mid-level managers and front-line supervisors accountable for preventing and/or responding to workplace harassment, including through the use of metrics and performance reviews.
- If employers have a diversity and inclusion strategy and budget, harassment prevention should be an integral part of that strategy.

Starts at the top. Most experts agree that changing the corporate culture needs to start from the top. In a June 2018 blog entitled Bringing Lessons from #MeToo to the Boardroom, the authors, Patricia Lenkov, founder and president of Agility Executive Search LLC, and Denise Kuprionis, founder and president of The Governance Solutions Group, note that in the wake of the #MeToo scandals, "Whether you are a member of the board of a public, private, or nonprofit company, procedures for addressing and preventing sexual harassment must be on your board's agenda. Directors need to do the right thing for employees, for customers, and for all stakeholders. The time for boards to act is now."

"Sexual misconduct" they suggest, "can be prevented, and prevention must be promoted at the top of the organization. While this is often articulated to be the case, the truth is usually more nuanced. Clearly, recent revelations highlight that we have lived in a culture where sexual misbehavior has been ignored, tolerated, and overlooked. Diversity in the boardroom can provide some mitigation in that it tends to curtail groupthink and group complacency. We need strong directors who will not be afraid to speak up or question unacceptable behavior within the organization they serve. It is easy to assume that directors, by virtue of their title, have the fortitude and wherewithal to do the right thing in all situations. But this is not always the case, and boards have a responsibility to interview and reference for these characteristics."

www.ingramcontent.com/pod-product-compliance
Lightning Source LLC
Chambersburg PA
CBHW062040270326
41929CB00014B/2487